How I Got My Wiggle Back

How I Got My Wiggle Back

A Memoir of Healing

Anthony Field
with Greg Truman

WILEY

John Wiley & Sons, Inc.

For general information about our other products and services, please contact our Customer Care Department within the United States at (800) 762-2974, outside the United States at (317) 572-3993 or fax (317) 572-4002.

Wiley also publishes its books in a variety of electronic formats and by print-on-demand. Some content that appears in standard print versions of this book may not be available in other formats. For more information about Wiley products, visit us at www.wiley.com.

ISBN 978-1-118-01933-7 (cloth); ISBN 978-1-118-16900-1 (ebk);
ISBN 978-1-118-16901-8 (ebk); ISBN 978-1-118-16902-5 (ebk)

Printed in the United States of America

10 9 8 7 6 5 4 3 2 1

*This book is dedicated to the memory
of my father, John Patrick Field,
and the inspirational chiropractors
who saved my life.*

Contents

Preface by Anthony Field

I don't care to look back too often.

Do you want to know about something that happened 15 years ago? You best ask my friend and Wiggles colleague Jeff Fatt. Curious about life a quarter century ago? My brother Paul is your man. It's not that I don't cherish all the fantastic milestones in life—my marriage, the birth of my kids, career achievements— or want to forget what my departed family members and friends meant to me, it's just that I prefer to focus on what's ahead.

Reflecting on more than 20 years with The Wiggles and nearly 30 as a performer is an odd sensation. After all, I'm still completely enveloped by it—nearly every waking minute—so to forensically evaluate that part of my life feels a little like writing a premature obituary.

If this book was only going to focus on the three decades and 8,000 shows I've played, I might be inclined to wait until I've done a couple of thousand more performances before settling into a comfy chair to celebrate having the best job in the world. But a sequence of events about eight years ago changed my story from being about the adventures of a children's entertainer to one of survival and, ultimately, personal triumph.

Illness and ailments used to define me. I was addled by theories and advice on what I needed to do to get back on track and my life-light was dimming. I had a litany of health challenges and they were defeating me, until through luck, desperation, and determination I found answers. They are contained in this book, not only as a way to explain what happened to me and focus on the people who helped me, but as a method of getting the word out about some incredible medicine and science that can change lives, millions of them.

I have a young family, a wonderful occupation, and I'm in the best shape of my life. In many ways, I feel like I've only just started—such has been my rejuvenation. I fully expect that there will be plenty more to add to the story of The Wiggles and my own jaunt in future years, but some tales need to be told before they're complete.

Preface by Greg Truman

If you're over five, without children and live in a dark cave you probably don't know that The Wiggles are the most successful pop band for preschool-age children of all time.

While studying to be a preschool teacher in Australia, Anthony Field (the Blue Wiggle) recruited a couple of fellow early childhood education students— singer Greg Page (Yellow), guitarist Murray Cook (Red), and a mate from his old rock 'n' roll group, keyboardist Jeff Fatt (Purple)—to record a little music for children, and the rest, as The Wiggles' character Dorothy the Dinosaur might say, is pre-history.

But for the record, they have dominated children's music in Australia for two decades and since the turn of the century have done a good job of making an Australian accent a common phenomenon in North American and British households with preschool-age children.

In 2006 and 2009 they received honorary doctorates from two universities for their work with preschoolers and in 2010, the four original members of the group were awarded one of their country's highest honors, the Order of Australia.

After 20 years on the road, The Wiggles play to more than a million paying customers a year and are still among the biggest live acts on the Australian, New Zealand, southeast Asian, British, and North American concert circuits. Touring North America several times every year since 2000, they frequently draw full houses in some of the largest venues in the United States and Canada and hold numerous box office records, including selling out 12 consecutive shows over a few days in 2003 at Madison Square Garden in New York.

Americans got to know the group through their mesmerizing music clips and top-rated cable television program, as well as regular appearances on network television programs such as NBC's *Today*. The illness-induced departure of The Wiggles' original lead singer, Greg Page, in late 2006 was front-page news in the *New York Times*.

Their profile has been helped over the years by a stream of stars publicly professing their genuine admiration—from rock legend John Fogerty to members of Metallica and Fleetwood Mac and sports notables such as Shaquille O'Neal. Celebrities have kids too, so Robert De Niro, Cate Blanchett, John Travolta, Sarah Jessica Parker, Chris Rock, and Jerry Seinfeld have all paid backstage homage to the band at the insistence of their children.

They have sold 27 million DVDs and CDs, more than a million children's books, millions of educational toys, and have created several successful television series. The group's production arm also has multiple "non-Wiggle" film and TV projects on screen and in development.

Consistently ranked among Australia's highest paid entertainers, The Wiggles have won nine Australian Recording Industry Association awards, the most recent for best children's recording in 2010.

In any entertainment genre—make that any business—The Wiggles register as a category one international success. The venture has brought the four original members of the group personal fortunes, a high level of creative satisfaction, expertise in a variety of performance disciplines, and a unique fame.

All this from what is essentially a cottage industry (gone mad). The grand notion of a wildly successful independent band is alive and well. The Wiggles was created by Field with a view to making music that didn't speak down to children and from his desire to be in control of his own creative destiny.

Yet, at the same time, while The Wiggles were managing to outperform the corporate powerhouses in the lucrative global children's entertainment market by making it their mission to be the best, developmentally sound musical fun a three-year-old could have, Field was engaged in a daily struggle to maintain his health and well-being.

As a long-term collaborator with The Wiggles and lifelong friend of Anthony Field, I was a proud spectator as the group blossomed into something truly magnificent—admired as much for what they have avoided becoming as for what they continue to achieve.

But my primary concern wasn't for the commercial or creative fortunes of The Wiggles. I was transfixed by Field's personal health struggles, which at times were life-threatening. Over the years he conducted a global search for answers to his challenges only to be thwarted time and again. Eventually, though, he found something extraordinary— not only solutions to his complex array of issues, but potential *fixes* for the ills millions of us deal with daily.

Fittingly, for the founder of a group that places special emphasis on simplicity and honesty in creative and business dealings, and that has battled to have their voice heard over the noise made by traditional industry heavyweights, the common sense, drug-free health innovations Field has embraced serve no one but the patient.

After 20 years, The Wiggles continue to thrive, but perhaps more astonishingly, so does Anthony Field.

Acknowledgments

How I Got My Wiggle Back was four years in the making and the result of a cooperative effort from scores of people on two continents.

To the Field and Truman families, especially our wives and kids, thanks for the love, patience, and perspective.

Doctors James Stoxen and Richard Gringeri not only provided the breakthrough medical material, they were involved every step of the way and were tireless in their commitment to the book. It wouldn't have been possible without their guidance.

Other medical friends and advisors include Johnny Petrozzi (BSc MChiro ICSSD) and Michael Sullivan (BDS (Hons) Syd.), and we bow to the inspirational memories of the great, late J. P. Field and Marie Truman.

Murray Cook and Jeff Fatt have been tolerant and blessedly grounded friends and colleagues over 20 years, while the entire Wiggles team including cast, crew, office staff, and production partners have gone out of their way to ensure the success of every venture including this one.

Special thanks to The Wiggles office maestros Paul Field and Kate Alexander who answered every question and plea for help in the construction of the book. Also our sincere gratitude to the hundreds of thousands of loyal Wiggles fans whose support means everything. We are especially grateful to the parents who shared their inspirational stories for these pages.

We're indebted to the professionals at John Wiley & Sons: Executive Editor Thomas Miller and workhorse editorial whiz Jorge Amaral; Senior Marketing Manager Laura Cusack, Associate Publicity Manager Mike Onorato, Senior Publicist Matt Smollon, and Senior Production Editor Richard DeLorenzo.

The unstoppable Lois De La Haba was at our side as agent and friend throughout and Marie Field was always on call, as she has been all our lives. Thank you.

PART ONE

My Musical Journey

1

The Early Days

People along New York City's Fifth Avenue stared at me. Dashing men and elegant women in heavy coats and tailored suits abruptly stopped strutting to look. They're certainly not shy in Manhattan. I remember giving everyone a big grin. Even the driver of a passing bus took a peek as he pushed his way past cabs and limousines.

Whoops, I was out in the road! Then back on the sidewalk. A blur of passers-by, New Yorkers and out-of-towners like me; all in a mad rush. It was making my head spin and my face hurt; I was probably smiling too broadly. I needed a little sit-down.

A crowd gathered. "Hmm, they're very quiet," I thought at the time. It did seem a bit odd that nobody wanted to talk. No one asked all the usual Wiggles questions: Is Jeff really that sleepy? Do you wear your blue shirt around the house? How many millions of years old is Dorothy the Dinosaur?

"Look!" I said to myself. There's a nice policewoman. One of New York City's Finest wants to talk. I wonder how old her kids are. Have they ever seen the show live? "What, officer?" I asked. "Homeless? No, I'm not homeless, just Australian." She didn't have a clue; maybe she didn't understand my accent. Maybe I should talk more slowly. "You know, Aus-tra-lia, Down Under . . . kangaroos?" (I think I even demonstrated a kangaroo hop.) She wasn't interested in small talk. She got serious with me real fast, suggesting I "stop dribbling, wipe the blood off your face, and fix yourself up."

Huh?

Then I realized those New Yorkers weren't staring at me because of The Wiggles—that was still a few years off. They were gawking, horrified, at a conspicuously disheveled middle-aged man who'd been staggering down the most revered street in Manhattan like an extra from a Wes Craven film. The Wiggles were in the early stages of our big American adventure and there I was, making an appalling spectacle of myself. "You see, Your Honor, it was the Novocain doing the talking."

We'd been touring like madmen in Australia and making frequent promotional visits to the United States but before charging off to America this time, I'd squeezed in a dental appointment.

Big mistake!

The pain was one thing: On the plane I'd been popping painkillers like my old Wiggles buddy Greg Page used to throw back candy (he loves Jelly Babies), but when I got to New York I had a full-blown dental emergency.

I consulted a local dentist who told me I needed immediate and extensive treatment to correct the shoddy work done in Australia. Without insurance to soften the heavy financial hit, I took a deep breath, jumped into the chair, and braced myself. Twelve thousand dollars and multiple procedures later, I stumbled onto the streets of Manhattan and made a scene that no one could miss.

The thing is, being in ridiculous soul-searing pain was normal for me at the time. I remember thinking I had just pushed myself a bit too hard. Everything would surely be all right in the next day or so. It was the sort of thing that was supposed to happen from time to time when you had spent decades on the road as a performer.

But it was not just a one-time event; in fact my problems were just beginning. Over the course of the next few years, I would lose nearly all of my teeth; battle hernias, back ailments, broken bones, food sensitivities, colitis, irritable bowel syndrome, potentially fatal infections, circulation issues, and exhaustion. To make matters worse, my deteriorating physical condition would accentuate an ongoing problem with depression I'd had for years. That Black Dog looms significantly larger if your body is fighting a losing battle.

Frankly, I was a basket case. I was too sick and miserable to enjoy the success that came The Wiggles' way. For a long period, I was taking pain medication daily. It took me a long while to realize that I wasn't living life to the fullest . . . I was just battling to get through the day.

Breaking Bad Habits

The Wiggles are on the road for up to nine months of the year. Don't get me wrong—it's great to see new places and meet new people, and I love my job. But it means spending countless hours on planes, buses, and in cars. We often go from one hotel room to the next, snacking on odd things at odd times, and eating at more greasy spoon diners in a few weeks than most people do in years. With two 90-minute shows most days on tour, it's easy to fall into a routine of unhealthy breakfast—vigorous performance— unhealthy lunch—vigorous performance—unhealthy dinner— bed (for some restless sleep, at the least).

And that's on a good day.

Even when we're back at home in Sydney, we're often in the studio until ridiculous hours, eating on the run, and exercising little, if at all. That kind of routine was okay back in the heyday of my first band, The Cockroaches. We played more than 300 gigs a year in every part of Australia; I mean, you feel like you can do anything when you're twenty-one. But, one day, I blinked and realized I was middle-aged and simply couldn't do it like I'd been doing it for years. What was immediately apparent to me, however, when I was mired in ill health, was that the solution to my situation *wasn't* immediately apparent!

I, like you, don't have hours a day to spend in a gym or to consult constantly with health gurus or muses. I have a demanding job and a young family and everything is a rush, a mad scramble. I habitually wake up at 4 a.m. and there are still not enough hours in a day. In the pages that follow, I will tell you in detail how small steps in the right direction led to meeting some remarkable people who had revolutionary ideas. With their help I was able to take giant strides down a positive path I didn't know existed.

The coolest thing about my subsequent transformation is that the medical and health insight I encountered and embraced is both astonishingly practical and available to millions of people who need it as much, if not more, than I. I'm not overstating it when I say I've come back from a position of utter hopelessness. Believe me. This shouldn't have happened. But, remarkably, it has.

When I took a step back recently and talked through my experiences with my friends and family, I found myself getting slightly annoyed. I'd spent tens of thousands of dollars, and a good chunk of what should have been productive waking hours over the decades, receiving treatment, drugs, and advice from prohibitively expensive doctors and experts—but in the end I discovered solutions weren't going to come from the people most of us trust implicitly.

I'm not here to sprout conspiracy theories or condemn individuals or corporations who make fortunes, effectively, by keeping us ill. I'm the son of a pharmacist who helped countless people so I'm aware of the fundamentally good intentions of most people in the medical community. I also continue to use medication from time to time for ailments including depression, so I'm not on an all-or-nothing bandwagon.

However, it's pretty clear to me that many traditional medical approaches have become compromised by an overt reliance on drug therapies and pain management. Those of us with chronic pain, or difficult-to-manage diseases such as diabetes, probably realize this better than anyone else. But real solutions seem to be such remote possibilities that it's hard to look beyond simply trying to put a lid on illness and injury.

Help Is Out There

My breakthrough began as a result of The Wiggles' treatment regime on the road. We are often in a new city every few days and over the last seven or so years we've come to rely on a group of different chiropractors to keep us going over the course of a tour. I won't even try to calculate the number of great people we've employed but there are two chiropractors, in particular, who not only guided me to great health but quite possibly saved my life.

James Stoxen and Richard Gringeri are innovative experts in their field. They are breaking down barriers in health circles as they demonstrate their methods. Armed with countless success stories, including mine, and a battery of commonsense treatments, they are making believers of specialists outside of the chiropractic community by the effectiveness of their drug-free approaches.

Before I met these gentlemen, I thought I had explored or been a guinea pig for just about every legitimate technique—traditional or otherwise—to counter chronic pain and/or temper the life-altering impact of a sensitive digestive system.

No.

What I was lucky to experience is profound and, until now, largely unheralded. This is *not* about deep-tissue or trigger-point massage (you chronic pain sufferers know what I'm talking about). This is *not* just another reminder to change your diet, watch what you eat, and how you eat it. What we have here are ways of looking at the human body that have been bypassed or not adequately investigated in the scramble to medicate.

Obviously I'm not a doctor, and to be honest my only contacts with chiropractors for many years were café encounters with my friend Dr. Johnny Petrozzi in Sydney, who loved coffee nearly as much as I did. He loved to bend my ear about how many conditions could be positively impacted by chiropractic care. But you know what? For the most part, I let it wash over me. I just didn't think a chiropractor could correct what countless other doctors failed to fix. Not to disrespect my buddy, but I was a traditional guy who thought your local plumber fixed your plumbing, your dentist checked your teeth, and your general practitioner cured physical ailments.

That was before I collapsed in a screaming heap.

If nothing else I've become an informed patient, having traipsed around the world consulting heavily credentialed doctors from distinguished institutions, looking for answers. (What I got, in the end, was a good idea of what didn't work and a constant stream of small white pills.)

In the midst of my own travails I also became acutely aware of the urgent need to contain some health issues that are running riot. Seeing literally hundreds of thousands of little people annually—some of them developing conditions that used to be largely confined to adults, such as chronic pain, obesity, depression, and diabetes—is a stark reminder that our traditional healers aren't winning the battle.

I didn't plan to be an advocate, but the fact that I'm still alive and kicking is testimony to the fact that there are solutions. There is a better way.

To put it simply, Dr. James Stoxen, *The Human Spring Doctor*, has a unique approach to eliminating chronic pain that has implications for tens of millions of people around the world. It all starts, literally, with putting the spring back into your step. Until recently, Doc James's approach had been largely a highly valued *secret* among entertainers and elite sports people. But I say don't let the rich, famous, and fabulous get all the breaks. It's time we let that cat out of the bag.

Similarly, Dr. Richard Gringeri, *The Human Engine Doctor*, has worked what amounts to medical miracles, for a lucky group of patients who for the most part had given up hope of reversing the impact of serious ailments. He helped me overcome a host of dietary issues. His innovative methods include advocating the ingestion of enzymes to help break down foods and eliminate toxins from the body. His holistic approach helped turn my health situation around, and now he is using it to tackle illnesses devastating entire communities, including the snowballing epidemic of diabetes.

Initially, I was just relieved the doctors seemed to help me overcome the chronic pain and decades of illness. But as I got more information about their ideas and methods, a kind of fog lifted and I could see blue sky for the first time in a long time. The results I experienced were immediate. In recent years I have maximized the benefits of my turnaround, developing advanced techniques and health routines that have helped me achieve elite fitness levels. I feel like I've won the lottery and have the numbers ahead of time for the next jackpot. And I really shouldn't keep them to myself.

That's why I wrote this book. It's not only a chance to tell my professional and personal adventures as an entertainer, but it's also about our common experiences of growing older, about the physical and mental challenges that face us all as we try to lead a *good* life. And it's about a personal commitment to change my life—not to discount the amazing help I've received from the incredibly innovative and inspiring people you're about to meet, but even they couldn't have fixed my problems if I wasn't prepared to change my life. The most important move I made wasn't implementing a new exercise regimen or making dietary refinements; it was opening my eyes and recognizing what I needed to do to keep my heart and soul happy.

I made changes that worked for me, and thank goodness I dared to do it. Today, I am almost pain free, certainly happier, and, at 48 years of age, healthier and fitter than I've ever been. I suspect similar changes will work for you as well. Make a healthy decision and listen to the best advice you can get.

That's how I got my Wiggle back.

Looking for the Yellow Brick Road

I come from a large family, the youngest of seven (four boys and three girls), who benefited immeasurably from the love and support of inspiring, witty, and wise parents. We were all pretty close in age so there was always someone to play and joke around with. A lot of stuff other children did with friends, I did with my siblings. We put on performances, played sports with and against each other, supported each other at school, and looked up to many of the same pop icons (there will never be another Elvis Presley).

Of course, looking back now, I was incredibly lucky; we were brought up to believe in and express ourselves. Laughing and performing were characteristics we developed early. Some of the best shows of my career were conducted in the family lounge room. We

Anthony, age 3.

The Field family in 1980: (from back) Marie, Maria, Patrick, John Patrick, John, Colleen, Paul, Anne, Anthony, and Bootlace the wonder dog.

were like a little tribe. Outsiders didn't just have to deal with one quirky Field, they had to contend with the whole bunch of us. Our mother was a talented musician and, at her urging, we all learned violin as young kids. We lived in a pretty tough part of western Sydney—seven kids in a three-bedroom house—and carrying a delicate instrument to school every day prompted a bit of teasing.

In our teenage years my three brothers—Patrick (the eldest), Paul (two years my senior), John (a year older), and I attended St. Joseph's College in Sydney, a famous all-boys boarding school my great-grandfather, an Italian immigrant, had helped build as a master stonemason. My dad had loved every moment of his education there and my brothers threw themselves into the vast sports program. (Joeys has produced more elite rugby union players than any other school in Australia.) I loved sports, but hated boarding at the school. Every day was painful in that regard. Yet, there was plenty to do and we devised ways to make life as easy as possible. For example, if you played in the school orchestra you got to miss three hours of homework time in order to rehearse your music.

Johnny and I played violin and actively avoided academic chores. We also started dabbling with guitars, trying to emulate our early rock 'n' roll heroes. We loved bluesy music performers such as Lightning Hopkins and blended it with our devotion to Elvis and the Rolling Stones. Paul discovered that if he sang rock 'n' roll on stage, girls would talk to him, so he did what anybody with access to two younger brothers would do and made us form a band. We recruited a couple of other St. Joseph's kids, including Tony Henry, who plays drums for us to this day, and made as much noise as possible, whenever possible.

The Cockroaches

We picked the name The Cockroaches because it had been an alias used by Keith Richards and the Rolling Stones in some unannounced gigs (Keith and The Cockroaches), plus it sounded

The Cockroaches at Trade Union Club in Sydney.

kind of punkish and that scene was blossoming in Sydney at the time.

School kept getting in the way of the band but we managed to learn a few songs. One of our first gigs was at St. Joseph's in 1979. Paul had convinced the Marist Brothers, who ran the place, to let us charge students five cents each for a lunchtime performance. All the money was to be donated to "the missions."

It would be fair to say that the performance was a success. Just as Johnny Cash mesmerized the inmates at Folsom Prison, so did The Cockroaches captivate the boys at Joeys. The testosterone-soaked atmosphere was teeming with hundreds of fine young Catholic lads hollering obscenities about a particularly unpopular teacher.

Paul was a motivated band leader and after leaving Joeys he started organizing gigs for The Cockroaches at some of Sydney's wicked pubs and clubs. The rest of us were still in school, so sometimes we had to sneak out to perform. We'd jump the old sandstone fences and scurry into Paul's car. Tony Henry's poor girlfriend used to lug his drum kit around for him. In later years, Paul was employed as an English and drama teacher at Joeys and had a particularly keen eye for potential escapees in his role as a dormitory master.

The music scene in Sydney in those days was vibrant, to say the least. Licensing laws were fairly relaxed so a lot of little bars would let bands squeeze into a corner and go for it. We built a following—which grew rapidly after I left school—at pubs such as the Heritage Hotel in Kings Cross, the Vulcan in Ultimo, and the Southern Cross (now the Strawberry Hills) in Surry Hills. We also played a lot of end-of-year school formals where we'd do our shtick and get to feed our faces on free food—something that helped us lure Jeff Fatt to the band.

"Fatty" was already a bit of a legend in the making, playing with his brother Hilton in a seminal Sydney rockabilly band called the Roadmasters. Hilton and Jeff also had a little PA-for-hire business. The white fiberglass-paneled speaker boxes (the washing machines) used by "Phattphonics" were ubiquitous in tiny city venues. They were versatile, easy to set up, and most importantly for The Cockroaches, cheap.

The PA was the "set and forget" variety, so inevitably, Fatty would turn up at the last moment, plug the thing in, and doze off while the bands had their way with the washing machines. Boredom was his toughest work challenge. One day we hired him to provide the PA for a performance in Newcastle, about 100 miles north of Sydney. He agreed to make the trip on the condition that he could play along on keyboards to stay awake. And that was the start of a beautiful three-decade relationship that has made him a very wealthy man.

However, securing Fatty's services on a regular basis wasn't a given. He was in high demand, playing with several bands. But in the end, The Cockroaches' regular gigs at school and university dances and formals made the difference. "Sometimes the lure to play at pubs wasn't much more than a slab of beer but that wasn't any use to Fatty cause he didn't drink," Paul said. "But with The Cockroaches, life was good . . . we'd often get fed at some of our gigs. Fatty liked that."

Fatty brought an element of musical sophistication to The Cockroaches and he was also the only one other than Paul to turn up on time. These days I'm a bit of a stickler for arriving early for shows, but punctuality wasn't my strong point back then. And my brother Johnny is still running late for a whole bunch of those Cockroaches gigs. However, John was a master showman—and still is.

The Cockroaches built a reputation for being a party band, partly on the strength of my brother's ability to be a lunatic on-stage. Whereas Paul was a picture of professional efficiency, Johnny would stop at nothing to get the audience revved up and involved. I remember one show at a venue on a beach in northern New South Wales when John decided to lead the audience—

hundreds of them—into the nighttime surf during an instrumental break in a song. He returned to the stage, dripping wet in his underwear, to complete the tune. But then again, half the crowd had stripped down and taken a dip with him.

Private Field

Over the years, we toured Australia countless times, playing at town halls, concert halls, pubs, parties, and Bachelor and Spinster (B&S) balls in every corner of the country. We sold a lot of records and packed venues everywhere. It was heady stuff.

Despite our workload, though, we didn't burn out like some of our contemporaries. We had a blast wherever we went, but we were kind of different from your average rock 'n' roll outfit. Drinking and drugs, for example, were never part of Cockroach culture.

Anthony and a friend at basic training.

Private Field and his parents.

In his capacity as a suburban pharmacist, my father, John Patrick Field, experienced firsthand, during more than one attempted armed robbery of his chemist shop, the devastating effects of drug and alcohol abuse. He used to counsel heroin addicts and dispense methadone, but some of the very same people he tried to help later confronted him with weapons, including guns and a machete on one occasion. (Several of them clearly hadn't thought through the repercussions of confronting the "mad" pharmacist who would routinely disarm the would-be robbers and more than once set off down the street in pursuit—waving the hapless bandits' weapons above his head.)

We kids got the message early and often about drugs. As a result, our idea of a wild night out on the road was largely restricted to eating like pigs at a local Chinese restaurant. The Cockroaches' old road manager Graham Kennedy, who was raised in a quiet, dignified, small-family environment, could only watch helplessly (and with mild disgust) as we three brothers and our boarding-school mate Tony Henry assaulted the fried rice, sweet and sour pork, or whatever was put within our reach during the nightly feeding frenzies.

Although I was on the road for most of my early adult years and had a penchant for Chinese food, I managed to stay pretty healthy. About the only thing we loved doing as much as performing was sports. We took every opportunity to pass and kick a rugby ball around or play impromptu cricket matches. My father had been an exceptional rugby player and rower. If nothing else, we inherited his competitive gene and some of those pickup games of touch rugby in bush towns sure were spirited!

It was a great existence. We were young, relatively successful, and loved what we were doing. Understandably, my older brothers were flying high, but I must confess, after a time I felt somewhat adrift. The Cockroaches was very much their project. Paul was the lead singer, chief organizer, and booker of gigs for the band and John was the main songwriter. I didn't feel like I could assert myself. What's more, I had struggled to keep a lid on perhaps irrational, but very real, feelings of inadequacy and depression ever since my days at boarding school in Sydney. For whatever reason, I was down on myself. Searching for a path, I decided to follow in the footsteps of one of my idols—Elvis. He'd joined the army and managed to look extremely cool doing it. So I signed on.

In retrospect, it wasn't a great move; it was a kind of career masochism to assert my independence in that way. I guess I must have still been feeling the effects of institutional life at school when I enlisted for that stint in the armed forces. I wasn't one for armed combat, any combat for that matter, other than the odd skirmish with my brothers, cousins, and friends on a sporting field. Occasionally I despaired about having made the commitment. I got by pretending to be a goofy, Gomer Pyle–like character, trying to be everyone's friend by making them laugh.

I missed my family terribly, especially when I was away for long periods of training. One time, after a long absence, I got the chance to head home for a family dinner. My brother John reminded me recently that I arrived unannounced in full battle uniform. With the family sitting around the dinner table I marched through the room without a word, returning minutes later to a standing ovation for the theatrical entry.

Fortunately in my last few years of service a position playing bagpipes for the army band helped me through safely and even allowed me to continue playing with The Cockroaches while fulfilling my military duties. I completed my time and hopefully didn't let anyone down before ending military service on July 14, 1985. I emerged with one "non-war wound"—a bad back, courtesy of military training.

Getting a Life

My search for a suitable career path intensified in my twenties after my army stint, even though the band continued to roll on successfully, becoming one of the biggest crowd-drawing groups in Australia.

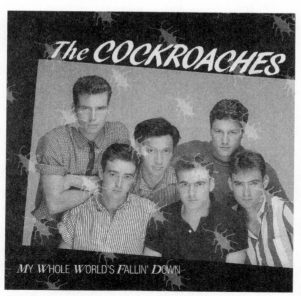

The Cockroaches: John Field, Phil Robinson, Jeff Fatt, Paul Field, Tony Henry, and Anthony Field.

Anthony and Johnny look on as Paul does The Cockroach in front of 50,000 fans in Sydney's Domain.

I tried a few things over the years; I even gave selling cars a shot. All I knew was that I wanted to throw myself into something and feel good about it. Unfortunately Anthony the Honest Car Salesman wasn't it. The boss sacked me on the first day when it became clear I was telling people *not* to buy certain vehicles. I also worked in a clerical position for the government, but just couldn't stop drifting off to sleep on the job.

My "Ah-Ha" moment came when I happened to accompany my sister Colleen on a trip to a Sydney university campus. She was contemplating an early childhood education degree, an idea that appealed to me too, though I had little idea about what it entailed.

I *could* tell you that I was immediately drawn to the cerebral challenge of study in an intriguing field. Indeed, I was quickly convinced early childhood teaching was my calling. But, let's face it, the initial attraction was the *women*—there were only about

Anthony in an advertisement in 1987.

ten guys in a class of three hundred in the first year of early child-hood education studies. Hey, I might have been depressed, but I wasn't stupid.

Soon, however, I saw past my hormonal reaction and recognized just how wonderfully right, on so many levels, a career teaching young children was for me. I'd felt restricted and hemmed in by the strict discipline at boarding school in my teenage years; early childhood education encourages the exact opposite by giving children the freedom to learn and express themselves. There is a very real arts-related flavor to some of the studies, too, which I connected with emphatically. I did a year at college and felt like a new man. "He's taken the Glad Wrap off his brain," my father declared.

The Cockroaches, however, were exploding in popularity and it became impossible to study while fulfilling my duties with the

Anthony with his mother, Marie, before he headed off to boarding school at St. Joseph's College, Sydney, in 1974.

band. I deferred university and threw myself back into music. Our first album went top ten and we played concerts to packed houses at least four nights a week. We kept our overheads low, traveling together in a minivan (which lost more than one windshield after some of our brotherly "discussions" became rather animated). We got to see a lot of the country, and, overall, the vibe was fantastic, but I just couldn't pull myself out of my lingering depression.

Unbeknownst to me then, a diet full of all the wrong things added to my malaise. It got to the point where I simply didn't want to tour anymore; I decided to take control of my life, my career, and my health. I was in my midtwenties and anxious to finish my education degree, and, in the back of my mind, I also had a plan to record music for children. I even suggested to the

The Field kids and their parents, John Patrick and Marie, in 1974. From left to right: Anthony, Paul, Anne, Patrick, John, Colleen, and Maria.

other members of The Cockroaches that we record an album for kids; they just looked at me as if I was completely loopy.

At the height of our success I had a brain snap or maybe it was a moment of inspiration and opted to take a backpacking trip to the United Kingdom. I can't remember a lot about the trip except that I didn't like the music everyone was listening to at the time in Australia and Britain—new wave and synthesizer-laced pop—so I made a tape of roots music and quality children's tunes featuring artists such as Canada's Raffi Cavoukian. I also put recordings of great kids' stories on my Walkman: Pat Hutchins's *Rosie's Walk* and Maurice Sendak's *Where the Wild Things Are*. Some of my cool backpacking mates got a shock when they asked to listen to the cassette I'd been engrossed in for hours on my hostel bunk.

When I headed back to Australia I was convinced more than ever I wanted to get into educating young children. However, The Cockroaches, despite being fiercely independent and basically shunned by the glamorous corporate record labels for years, were massively popular.

Anthony, age 5, joins his brothers and sisters at school in the winter of 1967. From left to right (youngest to oldest): Anthony, Anne, John, Paul, Colleen, Patrick, and Maria.

Out of necessity, more than anything, we had always organized our own shows and bankrolled our records and merchandising. At the time, record companies were signing musicians on the strength of their haircuts—even if the band couldn't attract more than a dozen people to a show. We, on the other hand, couldn't get any love from the major labels but would outdraw just about every group in the country.

Even when our first record went gold and we had ourselves a real manager, we were largely a self-contained outfit. Fatty would drive us to the gig; we'd be using Jeff's PA and we'd put a couple of friends on the door to collect a modest cover charge. The Cockroaches would play for an hour or two, laughing, singing, and dancing like lunatics and make a couple of thousand new friends in the process.

As my brother Paul said recently: "We felt like bank robbers." We'd jump back into the minivan after the gig and Fatty would drive us to a local motel where we'd race to a room and throw thousands of dollars on the bed. We learned a lot of lessons from The Cockroaches about keeping things simple, doing what you do for the right reasons, and believing in what you do. At times it was exhilarating, but I knew in my heart of hearts it wasn't what I wanted to do long-term.

Then something happened that changed my life and the lives of everyone associated with my family and the band.

The End of the Beginning

My restlessness had worsened after the release of the second Cockroaches album. It was a success, but we were disappointed with it, feeling we'd handed over control of the sound and makeup of the album to producers. Nevertheless, I toured heavily with the band to promote it, drawing big crowds in every corner of Australia.

As I continued to contemplate an exit strategy from The Cockroaches, tragedy intervened. When we were in North Queensland, thousands of miles from home, my brother Paul got a phone call. Dad answered the phone while Paul was in the shower. (Our father went on the road with us occasionally, usually to keep an eye on me; he knew I was struggling with depression. However, on this occasion, he was just there for the lark, reveling in our recent success.)

Dad had been staying in my room, but, as much as I loved him, he used to drive me nuts with his obsession about being ready for the day—he'd be up at dawn every morning (his nickname was "Hassles"), shaking me awake a couple of hours after our gig finished! After I booted him out he ended up bunking in with Paul.

Just as well.

There was no easy way to say it, and no easy way for anyone to hear it: Paul's seven-and-a-half-month-old daughter, Bernadette, had been found dead in her crib, a victim of Sudden Infant Death

Syndrome (SIDS). As horrifying as it was for us, it was obviously nothing less than devastating for my brother and his wife, Pauline. The gloom I had endured on the road with The Cockroaches was amplified a thousand times by his loss.

After the funeral and a period of mourning, Paul opted to soldier on with the band which was his creation, his livelihood, and his passion. But I could see nothing positive in returning to touring. I told the band I wouldn't—couldn't—do it anymore. For me, the choice was clear. I was ready to settle down, stay in *one* place, and become a teacher. But that decision was another cruel blow for Paul, who lugged The Cockroaches around Australia a few more times over the years in order to feed his family, sometimes with some of the original band members, other times not.

University Life

I went back to university to finish my degree. Suddenly, I was living a "normal" life. I still struggled occasionally with depression, but, overall, I was so much happier within myself. I relished going to college and I got into competitive sports again.

I played cricket with my brother John on Harry Phillip's mighty church league cricket team. John had been an exceptional cricketer at school. I loved cricket, but had opted to play basketball in high school, leaving the cricketing glory to my brother. But in my twenties, as I became more self-assured, I took up cricket with vigor. What I lacked in technique I'm sure I made up for in enthusiasm, although the back injury I sustained in the army probably became a chronic problem as a result of my efforts to become a cunning, medium pace bowler. We also had regular tip footy (rugby) epics. Mates from everywhere would turn up and we'd have full-blooded games. I'm not always proud of my on-field sporting persona—there were occasional disputes that could be heard several suburbs away.

Slotting into university life, I experimented with vegetarian-
ism and it was a big positive for me. I lost weight and felt one
hundred percent better than when I was on the road eating slosh
for breakfast, lunch, and tea. In my last year of university, I was
feeling healthy and in control of my destiny for the first time in
many years.

Having flirted with a few musical combinations since returning to the university, I decided to actually record some music for
children. I'd been struck—shocked, in fact—over the years at the
noninclusive way music for children was usually performed. Kids
often were made to sit silently listening to a pianist play (her back
to the audience), the traditional songs often featuring negative or
outdated lyrics and dealing with subject matter of no interest to
small children. At the other end of the spectrum some performers
would deliver "messages" to the children about global issues or
adult themes. Little ones don't get those concepts, their worlds
are far smaller.

Where was the fun? Where were the references to the simple
things that are so dominant in a child's life? Favorite foods, colors,
dancing, playing, nap time. And what's wrong with kids getting up
and grooving: squealing, screaming, and laughing through a performance? I wanted to explore alternate ways to write and perform
for young children, to ensure the music was for them, not just the
musician. Nothing complicated, snide, or condescending.

There were quite a few musicians among the very few men at
the college. There were plenty of great female musicians too, I
later found out, but initially at least, my shyness—yes, I was pain-
fully shy—precluded me from striking up relationships with many
of the women.

I already knew Greg Page, who had started studying early
childhood education at my urging. (True, I had suggested the
abundance of women doing the course was something for him to
consider.) "Pagey" was still a teenager and a few years behind me.
I was aware of his warm singing voice as he occasionally got up on

stage with the remnants of The Cockroaches and took on the responsibility of booking gigs for the band in the late 1980s.

Murray Cook ("Muz") was a mature-aged student like me. He'd had a career as a struggling rock musician in Sydney and we'd jammed in a university music room a few times. It's odd because we'd both played rock 'n' roll music for years, but because we were focused on early childhood education our jam sessions would usually revolve around songs like "Miss Polly Had a Dolly."

I had also gotten to know Phillip Wilcher, a talented classical musician and composer and the music assistant at the Institute of Early Childhood's music program. So when I decided to record a few tunes, I asked Pagey, Muz, and Phillip to come along. It turned out we needed another keyboardist to bolster the rock 'n' roll feel of the project, so I looked to my longtime mate from The Cockroaches, Jeff Fatt, who had "nothing on" that day.

We recorded a bunch of songs and I figured that would be that. But the other guys were quite taken with the idea of our little project becoming a full-time band and when the Australian Broadcasting Corporation took an interest in the recording, I suddenly found myself in yet another group. Wilcher left early on, but the others threw themselves into the project.

The Wiggles

My brother John had a major hand in our early songwriting efforts and performed with us regularly. Some of the shows were little preschool gatherings, other times—especially before the first album was released—Muz, Pagey, Fatty and I would hit the streets with John, busking around Circular Quay on the Sydney city waterfront and a few suburban shopping malls.

My brother was a fine emcee at busking events and Jeff and I had been doing them with him for years off and on. He used to churn out these instantly memorable pop tunes—some with complete lyrics, others featuring a chorus and a bunch of gobbledygook.

Murray, Greg, and Anthony and John Field at a Wiggles performance.

We'd sing and parade about, urging the crowd to join in. Shop-keepers were surprisingly tolerant as we'd snake conga lines through their businesses, 20 people dancing, singing, laughing, and occasionally knocking things over.

A couple of John's songs were absolute standouts: "Mr. Wiggles Comes to Town" was a favorite (as was "Hot Tamale," which we later changed to "Hot Potato"). When it came to looking for a name for the group, The Wiggles seemed to fit the bill. Johnny loved the freedom of the busks but found the dedicated preschool gigs a bit too "weird" so he left us to our own devices on stage, although he continued to contribute great songs.

Personally, I was content to record songs occasionally and con-centrate on my new career as an early childhood education teacher at Temple Emanuel in Sydney. But The Wiggles caught on like wildfire. Kids loved the music and the little show we put together. Before I knew what was happening, we were performing way too often for me to hold down a full-time job as a teacher. Reluctantly, I quit work and concentrated on The Wiggles full time.

Anthony prepares for a preschool performance.

I didn't recognize it at the time, but it was an amazing irony. I had left The Cockroaches after a decade so I could stop touring and get back to a normal life, in part to rebuild my physical and

Anthony at a show in 1991 as the crowds started to get bigger.

An early Wiggles calendar: Murray, Anthony, Dorothy the Dinosaur, Jeff, and Greg.

psychological well-being. But there I was—forming a band that was to become, literally, the hardest-working touring act in the country.

Faster than you can sing *yummy-yummy-yummy-yummy*, *fruit salad*, it seemed, I was back on the road. Don't get me wrong, it was wonderful doing something new and different for children. And the feeling you get playing in close quarters for little kids is just unbelievable—but I disliked touring. Besides, I had already been to every small town in Australia at least three times. However, I steeled myself because, as they say, the show must go on.

We adopted some of The Cockroaches' techniques, insofar as we kept our overheads low by traveling together everywhere in a minivan. The Wiggles were basically a self-contained operation. We had our own production gear that included props and costumes, and even sold promotional merchandise after the shows ourselves from out of the back of the van. Our old manager from The Cockroaches, Jeremy Fabinyi—bearing the scars from having to deal with the three volatile Field brothers—had reluctantly agreed to work with us as The Wiggles. He negotiated with the ABC to get us on the broadcaster's radar and helped us on our way as the recording was released.

We played preschools, crèches, malls, and a series of larger-scale shows featuring a group of performers called ABC for Kids. Murray recently reminded me of an ABC for Kids gig toward the end of 1991. "There were about 500 people there and it dawned on us that they were actually there to see us and maybe we should be doing these shows on our own."

Suddenly people started rolling up to performances in astonishing numbers. Mothers and fathers with kids in tow wasted no time getting involved—dancing along and participating in our simple conversations from the stage.

Before we released our second recording, we adopted Fabinyi's idea of wearing some kind of uniform on stage, which had kind of been our style with The Cockroaches (we had copied Elvis's look in "Love Me Tender"). The decision to emphasize color in The Wiggles was a no-brainer, considering our preschool-age audience, so it was just down to who would wear what. Murray had a red shirt so he was set and Jeff produced a purple garment that seemed to work. Both Pagey and I liked the idea of a blue shirt, but neither of us had anything suitable in our wardrobes so we met at a Sydney department store and literally raced to see who got the blue shirt.

Ha, victory! I'm not sure if Pagey ever really liked yellow.

Jeremy Fabinyi surprised us by moving on before our second CD was released. He had growing interests elsewhere in the music business and I think he knew I was fairly strident about what I wanted to see happen with The Wiggles, and figured we'd eventually butt heads. Fortunately, before his departure, he passed the reins to John Spence, who worked hard to book us all over the country.

Indeed, by late 1993 The Wiggles had already grown way bigger than anyone could have anticipated. Even the smallest country town shows would attract hundreds of children and their moms. It was immeasurably rewarding to get a sense that what we were doing was hitting the mark, but at the same time I was sick to death of being away from home. It got to the point where I would play poker machines every night in some club in whatever town we happened to be in just to have something to do. Within months, I was totally addicted to those bandits! Fortunately, my father raked me over the coals about it when he was with us on tour. I just couldn't wait for breaks in touring. Not only was it a chance to briefly recharge the batteries, but I could fully commit to devoting time to developing new songs or ideas for the group.

But we were drawing huge crowds to our shows and were quickly gaining exposure nationally through the media. Also the Australian Broadcasting Corporation's television network was playing our cheap and cheery film clips on a regular basis, helping to create a huge demand for our videos and tickets to our shows. Clearly this touring process was going to go on for a "few more years," I used to think, glumly.

Pretty early in our history, it seemed logical for us to develop a concept for a regular television program featuring The Wiggles. But children's TV was an extremely staid and cautious genre. The "gatekeepers" were experts who were not to be challenged or doubted.

At the back of my mind I was thinking that a Wiggles television show would mean I wouldn't have to tour as much (I was *so* wrong about that). So I was quite looking forward to the opportunity to meet with a leading producer, who reluctantly had agreed to work with us. Things didn't start well. I learned he had been telling people only the week before how much he disliked us (even though we had already sold hundreds of thousands of videos by this stage). I found myself disagreeing with just about everything he proposed. He made simple ideas complex and was anything but inclusive in the process. Nevertheless, he was the television expert, so, reluctantly we went ahead and agreed to make a pilot program with him. Suffice it to say, that pilot program will never see the light of day. He insisted we wear shorts, told us we weren't allowed to talk, and generally ignored everything we'd told him we stood for and were trying to achieve. It was yet another valuable lesson in maintaining self-belief and being true to what you do. Simplicity and common sense usually triumph.

Television would have to wait a few years (we eventually funded and produced our own series), so it was back to the road.

Zumo the Grump

My gloomy disposition and ongoing physical ailments made me a fairly poor traveling companion for my fellow Wiggles, and also helped me orchestrate the failure of a couple of romances I'd been in, including an engagement.

The Wiggles continue to take shape in the late 1990s.

Anthony in 1997.

The "cricket" back was chronically painful and I'd blown a few fuses with hernia issues. My vegetarian days were long gone, too; I was back to eating anything and everything on tour and it started to show around my waist. My self-image was taking a beating which, of course, gave my friends the perfect opening to play a trick on me.

We'd been traveling around the country and I'd been especially grumpy. It was the time of year when we looked at how we were going to package our merchandise and present ourselves going forward. I'd been concerned about my physical condition, having developed a spare tire around my midriff for the first time in my life. The other guys in The Wiggles were well aware of my hang-ups.

One day, when we were having a few photos taken, Jeff Fatt, my mischievous friend, quietly urged the photographer to take

Jacque the Shark fancies a nibble on Anthony's double chin.

An Elvis sighting on the show.

A shot from the 1997 Wiggles movie.

The Wiggles in a caveman bit.

The Wiggles on the road.

a few unflattering shots of me—pictures that accentuated my slight weight gain instead of concealing it. We were trundling around in the minivan a few weeks later when someone suggested we take a look at the photos. Fatty had strategically placed the "fat photos" at regular intervals in the pile we started to review. The other guys watched me carefully as I reviewed the snapshots. I was horrified, but couldn't bring myself to say anything right away. After a while, however, I couldn't resist. I blurted that I looked like a sumo wrestler, but quickly pointed out that it's probably a good thing for kids to see entertainers who aren't necessarily the skinniest people in the world. I was deadly serious, and the guys kept a straight face for a long time, but they all burst out laughing eventually. They detailed the setup and quickly assured me I wasn't in any way obese. But that didn't stop them from embellishing my sumo wrestler rant from then on. In the sometimes strange world of The Wiggles, we butcher the language occasionally by using a "Z" to start words and sentences. So my sumo reference became "Zumo," and that became a nickname that has stuck with me over the years like cream buns stick to the hips.

In spite of my personal dissatisfaction with life on the road, the hard work was paying off for The Wiggles. It seemed the tradeoff for being successful was dumping any intention to spend time renewing mind, body, and spirit. We'd tour nine months of the year, and the other three we'd be recording or writing material.

My life was the minivan, country hotels, bush town cuisine, side-of-the-road fried stuff, and the dark atmosphere of recording studios. The lifestyle was a necessary evil, I thought at the time, and I really couldn't complain to anyone. For the most part, I was engrossed in developing songs and other Wiggles projects for children, including videos, movies, and television shows. That was the part of my life I loved.

When I was "up" at show time, or working on material and ideas, I was flying high, but when the toll of the road, my diet, and my tendency toward depression took hold of me again, I tumbled down. Then the death of a schoolmate of mine, "Cow" Costigan, sent me plummeting.

By the mid-1990s, The Wiggles were among the biggest acts in the country, but I was frequently gripped by anxiety, sadness, and negativity. I don't remember exactly when I hit rock bottom, but I do recall being in a dark place psychologically. I was suicidal. I know that seems illogical. It is illogical, I had a job I loved and we were successful. But at the time my desperation and depression were very real and debilitating in the extreme. I had been on the road for fifteen years, my health and fitness swinging like a pendulum. My love life was in tatters, my self-esteem nonexistent.

Ironically, I was laughing and smiling on stage, relishing bringing joy to preschool-age kids. But during my downtime, alone with my thoughts, I'd flit between feelings of inadequacy and disgust with myself for being selfish—letting my moods interfere with my otherwise charmed existence.

I was so ashamed I couldn't bring myself to talk to anyone about it, which of course, makes matters much worse. Fortunately, Dad was watching. One day, quietly, deliberately, he took me aside. He didn't need specifics; he didn't need me to explain anything. He simply told me we would overcome whatever it was that was pinning me down.

It was a wonderful act of love and typical of my father. Dad found me professional assistance. It kept my head above water.

Depression continues to be my unwanted companion from time to time, but it no longer holds me hostage. We're winning, Dad.

2

America Beckons

What's in a name?

Quite often it's alliteration if you're talking about animal characters in children's entertainment. You know, Bugs Bunny, Maisy Mouse, or Dimity the Dinosaur.

OK, so Dimity isn't the dinosaur on everyone's lips. But consider for a moment, if you will, what might have happened if that nice lady in Maine had opted to continue to perform to a handful of kids under the name Dorothy the Dinosaur. That's right, in America at least, our rose-eating green and yellow dinosaur would have been renamed Dimity—on every recording, on every piece of merchandise.

Way back in 1996, even before we'd made meaningful connections in America, it occurred to us that if we were ever to venture to the U.S. it would be in our best interests to ensure the "path was clear" in terms of trademarks and copyrights. We found out that someone in Maine had been clever enough to register the name Dorothy the Dinosaur, so we were faced with the very real prospect of having to rename our favorite singing and dancing reptile if we did set foot in the U.S. Fortunately we reached an agreement with the woman, securing the right to introduce Dorothy to America in the (unlikely) event we headed over. Due to legal constraints I can't talk extensively about that arrangement, but it's fair to say we had to dig deep for the deal. It left a few of our associates scratching their heads—we had no announced or unannounced plans to head overseas, so why opt to pay out?

I guess it's a good example of the way we've always done things. Our focus is always on the playroom before the boardroom and our instinct has been to trust our knowledge as early childhood educators and entertainers to propel us in the right direction, rather than develop elaborate, long-term business and strategic plans.

We didn't know if America was going to be an option, but we had developed a fairly unshakable belief in our approach and knew that much of that confidence was derived from our success in maintaining our core values and continuing to be mindful of what worked for our audience. It was kind of an all-for-one and one-for-all approach. If we decided to do anything overseas it would have to be on our terms and anchored by the same concept we'd poured blood, sweat, and tears into over the years.

That's why, for example, against all advice, we opted to keep our show simple when we first toured the U.S.—no expensive props or effects, just the four of us and the characters, singing and dancing, pretty much as we did when we started in Australia a decade before.

It's why we walked out on the British entertainment industry enfant terrible who proposed The Wiggles in the U.K. should be made up of local performers singing songs the Brits "could relate to." And it's why we didn't sell our concept or its ownership to anyone, including interested global companies. We remain hands on, to this day, with every major decision.

We obviously carefully consider what we do and we do listen to advice, but prefer to act rather than pontificate. We make decisions by consensus, though there are no executive boards or shareholders for us to answer to, just ourselves. We don't have to plan a weekend away or spend a day behind locked doors to mull a decision. In fact, quite a few key projects have been launched during a brief pause in an X-Box game on our tour bus.

We make mistakes too, but when you're doing things for the right reasons it inoculates you, in a way. As my brother Paul says, looking back to a time when America was just getting to know us, we'd spend a considerable amount of time trying to decide if, for example, we needed to change a line in Dorothy's onstage dialogue, but only take a few minutes to approve the purchase of a building.

It's fair to say ours is not your regular "corporate culture"—I only recently stopped bringing pillows to business meetings, though I still find discussing fiscal matters a dirge and start glazing over when the discussion turns to "what could be."

The Red, Purple, and Yellow Wiggles

Procrastinators and pessimists aren't thick on the ground in Wiggle World, though that's not to say we're all bright, happy, and shiny optimists. On the contrary, all of us—the four original members— were anything but self-assured as kids (which is probably why we love to be part of the process of empowering children).

As previously discussed, I've always struggled with shyness, while Fatty and Muz were quiet retiring kids who became intelligent and considerate adults. And as a teenager Pagey says he used to do his best not to stand out in the crowd.

I knew pretty early on with The Wiggles that I had finally found a natural way to connect with an audience. My pharmacist father had it as a drug and alcohol counselor and lecturer, and my brothers Paul and John found it with The Cockroaches. While it didn't immediately solve my other personal challenges, it brought an element of balance to my roller-coaster life.

Additionally, as luck would have it, we also achieved a great balance within the group. Pagey's mellifluous voice is the perfect children's music instrument, Muz has a great understanding of what's developmentally appropriate, and Fatty's incredible musicianship and gentle persona have great appeal for children. I suppose I bring a certain energy to the process and I love constructing the look and sound of the show.

We also learned to make the most of our individual quirks and talents and developed a fairly effective system of on-the-run checks and balances over the years. I've always been anxious to get on with things, while Muz and Pagey were good at playing devil's advocates. Fatty, probably stemming from years of being caught between the three constantly warring brothers in The Cockroaches, is a master at the art of fence-sitting.

Murray, the King of Guitars.

Muz moves more cautiously than I do—someone has to. It used to drive me nuts. I'd think he wanted to kill everything off, but I came to understand his method was different from mine, and for good reason. I believe we've both got good radars but Muz's approach is less instinctive. On more than one occasion he's pointed out potential problems when all I could see was the upside.

This has been important in preserving the good name of The Wiggles (people say the "brand," but I just can't bring myself to think in those terms). For example, years ago a large fast-food outlet wanted to sell a particular line with The Wiggles' name on it. I was OK with it: The food was nutritionally sound and we wouldn't be actively hawking the product, but Muz could see a complication. He made the point that kids are already bombarded with fast-food options and advertisements and merchandise. Even if the product is good, parents probably would prefer if their children weren't lumping The Wiggles and fast food together.

Like me, Murray had real-world experience in early childhood education and probably would have been content to continue teaching and perhaps move into an academic role in the field. He knows his stuff and is simply great with children.

I remember a Sydney concert a few years ago in front of about 8,000 kids. At all of our concerts we regularly head into the audience to say hello to the children—sometimes Fatty covers miles each performance, running around the auditorium several times. On this day we waved, smiled, gave occasional high fives, stopped here and there for a quick photo, but stayed on the move for the most part to avoid getting stuck in the heart of the crowd.

After a trek that took Murray to nearly every corner of the venue he arrived back at the foot of the stage and gave one last smile and wave as he prepared to rejoin the rest of us. But before he could, a young boy, maybe eight years old, who had been seated among a number of physically disabled children, ran over to him and in one unabashed and glorious moment wrapped his arms around the waist of the nearly 6 ft.4 in. Red Wiggle.

Momentarily surprised, Murray looked down and saw the little guy. Gently, he hugged him—an embrace of such spontaneity and tenderness several members of the audience told me later they shed a tear at the sight. The boy, his head having been buried in Muz's stomach, looked up at his hero and gave him an appreciative smile that seemed iridescent in the wash of the stage lights. Murray looked him in the eye and beamed back. A final, mutually affectionate squeeze and Muz headed back to the stage. Everybody who witnessed the exchange knows he made that boy's life a tiny bit better. And, no doubt, the feeling's mutual for Murray.

Pagey also was a perfect fit in more ways than one. His big friendly smile and easy stage manner made him an engrossing sight for the kids and adults. He has an authoritative, though not overbearing, tone when he speaks to children and is a relaxed and clever emcee.

Greg Page during a performance.

Pagey plays it straight opposite Anthony.

While the other Wiggles and the characters can be playful and occasionally mischievous, Pagey was always the perfect straight man for The Wiggles. When we started out, Greg had the advantage of being much younger than the rest of us, especially Fatty. He was only 19 when we released our first recording and the touring was a complete novelty for him. He loved every moment of being on the road in the early years and was a buoyant and involved member of the troupe—and as a result was probably the target of my foul moods more often than the others. I also concede I was somewhat dictatorial in those early days.

One time, in a tiny Australian town, we were setting up equipment for the show. I seem to recall Pagey was particularly spry. I, on the other hand, was probably in the midst of yet another relationship implosion. Even early on, the other guys could recognize when I was primed for a "brain snap" and would feed the beast, so to speak. I grumpily tinkered around with a few stage props, one of them a little drum kit I was going to play in the show.

Pagey reminded me recently of what happened next. I had just set the drum kit up between the house speaker and the audience when the Yellow Wiggle said, "Oh, you probably shouldn't set it up there everyone will hear the drums not the sound." He was probably right, but it's safe to say Greg was interested in pushing my buttons that day in addition to preserving the sound quality for the show. But I bit, and my inner Keith Moon was exposed. I picked up the little kit and flung it across the stage and snarkily asked, "Is that better? No one will hear it now."

Fatty was the instigator of more than one trick to get me to blow my top over the years, but his quiet demeanor and ability to pick his moment to step in and contribute, to either practical jokes or business decisions, makes him invaluable company on the road. I'm sure I wouldn't have been able to get through 20 years of touring with The Wiggles and another eight or nine with The Cockroaches if it weren't for Jeff's calm approach to everything that came our way.

Sleepy Jeff and Anthony on stage.

His willingness to be the chauffeur of the minivan during the Cockies years was probably as much a desire to stay away from the heated brotherly conflicts as it was a genuine enjoyment of steering us between country towns.

Fatty was a "bush" kid himself—from the northern New South Wales town of Casino, where he first learned to let his keyboard do most of the talking. When I called him in 1991 to see if he could come and help out with our little children's music project I was putting together he asked, "Will it take long?" At the time he was very busy renovating his house and going to the beach. As it turns out, Jeff enjoyed our music and our approach (and the prospect of free food at some gigs).

As he had been with The Cockroaches, initially, he served the role of being a musical backbone for The Wiggles. However, we couldn't hide our shy friend on stage in front of thousands of small children—we had to somehow get him moving and develop his onstage personality.

If you haven't seen The Wiggles, you might not know that Jeff, the Purple Wiggle, is the sleepy one. (I'm the hungry one.) It's the product of a simple audience participation and interaction gag we've done since the start of the group. Someone incongruously falls asleep on stage and the kids notice. They want to let us know. We thank them and ask them to be sure to let us know if it happens again, by calling out "wake up." In the very early days each guy in the group had a turn at falling asleep, but when Fatty did it it was a perfect fit!

"It gave me something to do," he said. It's a simple stage tactic that has helped endear Jeff to audiences around the world. And, for a time, gave some young men the idea of noisily accelerating their cars near his home in Sydney while screaming "Wake Up Jeff!" at 3 a.m.

Jeff is living proof of the benefit of a good diet, good genes, regular exercise, the absence of alcohol, and a considered approach to the problems and challenges some of us—er, me—feel swamped by on a daily basis. At 58 he is one of the healthiest people I know—of any age. Over more than 20 years he never missed a show with The Wiggles due to illness. Believe me, that's an achievement of epic proportions. What Cal Ripken Jr. did in baseball, Fatty has emulated in live children's entertainment.

Last year, however, "Iron Man" Fatt's run came to an end. Shockingly, he was diagnosed with an irregular heartbeat that required a pacemaker—proof that he was human.

Fatty popped into the hospital while we toured the U.S. and got his new piece of equipment. Soon after, he hit the stage again and looked set to perform without another break for a couple more decades.

With the surprises and occasional turmoil that engulf a touring band you expect to be distracted sometimes, maybe even negatively impacted, especially by those who circle, waiting to take a bite of your business, but not Fatty. No doubt there's as much turmoil and conflict in Jeff's life as there is in the lives of some others, but here is a man on whom the gods seem to smile.

On a rare day off recently, Fatty was pottering about his house when he saw me in a boat on Sydney Harbor with a few of our Wiggles cast. It was an immensely beautiful Sydney day—a mind-bogglingly clear, blue sky, gentle swells, and a delicate, cooling breeze. A perfect day for a dip. So Fatty wanders down to the shoreline, gives us a wave, plunges into the water, and heads toward our boat.

The Purple Wiggle was preoccupied executing his Australian crawl with the precision of Ian Thorpe so he didn't notice when we started jumping up and down, frantically trying to get his attention. There was a shark swimming under the boat.

But Fatty was too focused on the task at hand to notice. As we scoured the waters to track the man-eater, Jeff nonchalantly climbed onboard, ready for a day's outing. "What?" he asked, when confronted by his friends and colleagues, looking like they'd seen, well, a shark.

Lessons Learned

There are a few things Jeff Fatt and I learned from our time with The Cockroaches:

1. Trust your creative and business instincts and maintain control of your destiny.
2. Don't order the fish in country towns on Sundays.

From The Wiggles' point of view, point one is probably more important, although lesson two comes in handy, particularly if you find yourself in a landlocked community.

The single best thing we did from a business perspective was to ensure the four guys in the group had ownership and creative control over everything, from touring to recording to ventures in television and film. Sure, sometimes we needed partners to make things happen, including great companies such as Disney, Roadshow, and ABC Australia, but we kept a tight grip on what we did because we knew we were doing something right.

That caused occasional heartache and outright confusion at times, as the scale of our little singing and dancing business exploded in the 1990s, but we worked to maintain a clear focus on our calling to provide developmentally appropriate entertainment for young children and make our performances the best they could be.

It had been so much easier in the early days when we worked out of the back of the minivan. We'd unload our gear, sing our songs, sell nice people our CDs and a few little knickknacks, then head out for an unhealthy dinner somewhere. The money would come in, the money would go out. You could track everything. It was a simple but satisfying process. We made adjustments over the years to better deal with the growth of the business. We continued to strive to keep things simple, regardless of whether we were bringing in thousands or millions of dollars. We trusted people we knew and made sure we got to know people we had to trust. But after a half-dozen years on the road in Australia, it became clear we had done just about everything we could—most of them at least twice.

Annually from 1995 our videos had been among the biggest sellers of any genre in Australia and topped the children's sales charts. We played to more people in concert (and more concerts) than just about any other touring act in the country and had made a successful feature film and a television series. We saw no reason why we couldn't do what we had done in Australia on a regular basis overseas. Maybe we were naïve but why complicate matters? We knew what we were doing was positive and enjoyable for kids, and their parents seemed to get it too.

However, it was going to mean a big commitment, not just in time, but in heart and soul. Basically we'd have to start all over again. Touring and promoting ourselves in several different countries, while still trying to squeeze in existing writing, recording, and performance obligations. I'd had enough of being on the road years before, but here I was contemplating doubling my workload. We quickly found out that the more committed we became to overseas expansion, the greater the professional demands on our time and the more difficult it became to reverse or at least contain the health challenges that had started to dominate my life.

And I wasn't alone. Every member of The Wiggles, except the oldest one, Fatty had been hit hard by either injury or illness. Our show had become extremely taxing physically, with active choreography running right through each 90-minute performance. But that was a double-edged sword. It helped us keep some of the pounds off when we were on the road, but asked a lot of our less-than-finely-tuned bodies.

I had to drop out of a tour in New Zealand and stayed behind as the guys played Hong Kong because I had excruciating chronic back pain, terrible toothaches, and was getting sick regularly. Even when I pieced myself together enough to go out on tour, I battled bad reactions to a number of different food types. There were countless times when I'd end up doubled over with stomach pain.

I visited chiropractors, general practice medical doctors, alternative healers, and Feldenkrais practitioners. Sometimes they helped, but the litany of health problems ballooned, especially when we were on the road. Around that time I became acutely aware of the link between my physical and emotional well-being. One feeds the other. My nickname was Zumo but perhaps it should have been yo-yo. I was up and down with unrelenting regularity.

Over the years I'd routinely leaned on my dad for support, but now the dear fellow was struggling himself, the victim of a massive stroke. Hassles always had been a step ahead of me. He could read me better than I could read myself and he urged me to be honest and open with him, saying nothing shocked him "except electricity." He was still aware of what was going on around him, but had lost the ability to fully express himself. It's hard to describe how devastating that was for him and us. He had been a razor-sharp wit and raconteur his whole life, but here he was barely able to put a sentence together.

Gradually he pulled back from the front line of life. My confidant was gone.

When he ended up in the hospital after a second stroke, everyone in my family put their lives on hold. The Wiggles had been making plans to try our luck in the U.S. and the U.K. but I found it difficult to keep my mind on the job. Dad didn't have much to say in his final few days but at one stage he looked me in the eye, grabbed my mother, the beautiful Marie Field (nee Richie), and garbled, "This is love. This is love."

I knew what he was trying to impress on me. While my career was booming, my personal life was a mess. I dated some truly wonderful women, but my relationship track record was appalling.

J. P. Field died on May 7, 1998.

Setting Priorities

In more ways than one, Dad's death ushered in a new phase of my life. As The Wiggles tried to prioritize international targets, I also worked on personal goals. But there was barely time to contemplate anything other than the professional road ahead. The U.S. and the U.K. beckoned as a few of our business partners expressed an interest in giving us a leg up.

We played concerts at Disneyland in California and at a variety of theme parks in the U.S., including a stint as the opening act for a relaunched version of *Captain Kangaroo*, an old American children's favorite. The performances opened our eyes to the possibilities and reinforced our belief that we were doing something very different from what America was used to. A couple of the large entertainment companies just didn't get us, but a few significant supporters started to appear. That was not the case in the U.K., where the rainy weather combined with poorly planned and promoted performances to make matters glum. And let me state for the record, I was a complete misery when we first visited those shores.

What's more, the entertainment executives charged with promoting us oozed condescension and disinterest. More than once, in the early years of our contact with Britain, we had stressful and infuriating disagreements with a few influential people who seemed content to be critical without being in any way constructive. It was quite clear we were expected to bow to their "standing" in the industry. I had no problem with that, except they failed to bring anything other than their reputation to the table.

We ended up playing a mixture of summer camp concerts in remote areas, usually staying in rundown roadside inns during those first visits to Britain. Initially, at least, it just didn't seem worth it. It was excruciatingly lonely on the road and more than once I just felt like throwing in the towel. My fellow Wiggles were saints in the way they tolerated my dark moods.

Making matters worse, I wasn't making great inroads in my quest to get my act together in terms of relationships. In fact, it got to the stage where I simply didn't think I'd ever have a permanent partner and I told my mother I didn't expect to ever marry. I'd just have to content myself with my surrogate family—my posse of snapping yappy mini fox terriers back home in Sydney.

Somewhat ironically, I was named Australia's Bachelor of the Year in 1999. Little did the organizers of the annual *Cleo* magazine–sponsored award realize I was a terrible catch at the time—depressed, disillusioned, and overweight. I'm pretty sure I'm the only guy with a spare tire around his waist, suffering from clinical depression, to receive that honor.

It was flattering in a way and probably the last sort of recognition I expected to receive. As I mentioned earlier, I'd always been intensely shy around women. As a kid I used to get my brother Paul to call girls I fancied and things hadn't improved much in my adult life, even into my 30s. Plus, as a children's performer, you feel a certain obligation not to be seen abusing the privilege kids and their parents bestow on you to be a trusted and responsible "friend," so public cavorting, however benign, isn't a great idea. It made even innocent social interaction with women difficult sometimes and on occasions, especially after the bachelor thing, downright embarrassing.

I remember once in Perth, Australia, I was surrounded by a group of young women teachers in a nightclub insisting I prove, in the crudest possible way, I was "straight." I managed to talk my way out of that one, but that kind of silliness tended to push me back into my social shell and in the long run probably helped accentuate my loneliness.

The good thing was that there was so much work to do, writing new material, recording new and rerecording old songs (predominantly for North America), fine-tuning the stage show, and planning for tours and television. I didn't mind the workload—that was a blessing of sorts—but the touring got me down.

Riding on Barney's Back

We had ongoing obligations in Great Britain but quickly came to the conclusion that it would be more productive at that time to start concentrating our efforts in the U.S. We had struck up a relationship with Texas-based Lyrick Studios, the driving force behind Barney the Dinosaur in the U.S.

We were still barely a blip on the entertainment radar in North America, but thankfully Lyrick "got it." They knew what we were trying to do and the way we were trying to do it. Unlike some companies and individuals we interacted with, Lyrick had done its homework, testing our material with kids and plotting a modest but sensible strategy to help lift our profile. The company's head of marketing at the time, Sue Beddingfield, had a bit of a mantra we could relate to. She used to say, "If people see them, they'll love them." From years of experience, we knew that was the truth.

Children are remarkably astute. They have better entertainment and information radars than most adults and are brutally honest about what they like and what works for them. Young children identify with relevant concepts, and enjoy being entertained and being part of the entertainment. They are willing to commit to interacting if you are direct, inclusive, and positive.

But we had to get in front of as many people as swiftly as possible in order to get that U.S. "love affair" going. It came down to being prepared to do the hard yards to get exposure in North America, and hauling ourselves out of our Aussie comfort zone. In 1999, for one week we would be playing to 8,000 people in a Sydney concert and the next week to twenty people at a performance in a shopping center parking lot in a small U.S. city. I distinctly remember a rather painful promotional appearance at a Blockbuster video store in California that drew four people (thanks for coming, you guys, hope you're still fans). Another time in Minnesota, at the Mall of America, we got about a dozen people over several hours, and half of them were our rent-a-crowd friends from Lyrick.

But gradually things started to improve. Persistence does bring rewards. In-store promos became big local events and there was a kind of buzz from the kids we recognized from our early days in Australia. They knew the songs and our stage characters and were clearly tapping into the simple subjects, objects, and issues we raise in performance.

We followed a little gig at the bandshell in New York's Central Park that had attracted about 50 people (most of them dog walkers) with a full-blown concert there for 400 a few months later. Unfortunately the comings and goings between the U.S. and Australia weren't great for my health. I'd sought medical help for stomach ailments, though I usually got nonspecific advice to "improve my diet" or, occasionally, to "rest more." But I knew there was something more significant going on as I'd often spend good amounts of time experiencing the wonders of restrooms in various cities around the world.

My back and hernia issues continued to flare too, in part because I was piling on the pounds. No Zumo joke here, I was getting to a stage where I was a genuine heavyweight. I actively avoided bathroom scales, but I was probably about 30 pounds larger than I should have been. The routine usually went something like this: haul my rotund self out of bed, grab my yet to be unpacked suitcase, race to the airport, use the airport toilet for an embarrassingly long period, and then limp onto the plane. Once uncomfortably seated, I'd count the minutes until the plane was airborne long enough to allow me to use the onboard facilities. (I accumulated countless frequent flyer miles in the toilets of aircraft.) Eventually, I'd try to sleep, oftentimes, stupidly with the aid of sleeping tablets or painkillers. On arrival, I'd use the airport toilet, before heading to the hotel where I'd tumble into a room— maybe eat something despicable—and wait to fulfill concert or promotional obligations.

Glamorous, huh?

I also had regular toothaches and other oral woes, but at the time they barely registered as a blip on the radar as I tried to cope with the other ailments and keep depression at arm's length. I just wanted to get through each day as something resembling a regular functioning human being.

I was a toxic mess, topping off the cocktail with ongoing poor nutrition and irregular sleeping patterns, ensuring that my physical frailties would be compounded with binges of physical exertion, as I'd bound onto the stage to dance, jump, and roll around without adequate warm up or even a semblance of a training program.

Talk about a walking time bomb.

But, at the time, I didn't feel I had the time to recover from illness, or even go to the doctor in some cases. Ignorance is not bliss, but it's convenient sometimes. I knew I had issues, but if I kept myself busy I could avoid thinking about it.

The progress we were making in the U.S. reinforced the idea that we had to do even more. Lyrick was terrific, pushing to get us in front of kids around the country. The Lyrick folks were perfect partners because they left most of the creative stuff to us, although I do recall one period of extended discussion about an issue that had been a persistent problem for many Australian acts trying to break in overseas—our accents. To be honest, we hadn't given it much thought, although we were confused about the fact that cabs in the U.S. often seemed to take us to the strangest places despite our best efforts to give clear and concise directions. (I'm still baffled about how you mistake "the Bronx" for "Brooklyn Heights.")

Sue Beddingfield and her team seriously considered packaging us with an Australian-American dictionary, or at least a glossary of terms. Fortunately, not too much time was spent on conquering the issue of being separated by a common language. As Murray, the astute Red Wiggle points out, toddlers don't have the same hang ups as adults. Preschoolers are in the act of formulating their communication skills so they simply adapt to different pronunciations of common words or come to terms with the context in which things are presented. Regardless, speaking "toddler" is a skill we mastered pretty early.

Lyrick, to our relief, dispensed with the idea of explaining our accent to America, while clinging to the belief that with exposure to kids, success would come. It was a tiny masterstroke that eventually gave us the opportunity to get in front of children, en-masse.

Barney was Lyrick's big act. We gratefully accepted an invitation to play a few songs during the ten minute intervals in the touring show featuring the purple dinosaur. (Unfortunately we had to leave our own prehistoric costume character, Dorothy, at home. Too many dinosaurs on stage can be distracting.) It was great fun and we could tell the connection was being made with Barney's massive audience. Lyrick followed this up by putting one of our songs on a Barney video and *that* pushed us over the edge.

The Wiggles video sales in the U.S. took off in 2000, with the first two North American releases, *Yummy Yummy* and *Wiggle Time*, jumping into the Amazon.com top ten. Then, the huge retailer, Wal-Mart, agreed to stock us. To use a technical term, things went nuts in the U.S. and Canada.

We got a good gauge of the progress we'd made on another tour with Barney (this time Dorothy was allowed to join us), and during a string of in-store appearances. In some of the same places where it had been so quiet six months before you could hear crickets chirping, it was jolly mayhem.

In 2000, we'd toured Australia, New Zealand, Hong Kong, the United States, and the United Kingdom, a few of them several times. We were starting to see the kind of results we'd worked for. However, my health situation was nothing short of calamitous. I had started missing shows and literally staggered onto stage on several occasions. But we were busy. So busy. We had no time for anything other than work.

Hey, what's that ticking sound?

The joys of eating on the road.

The whole Wiggles gang, including Henry the Octopus, Captain Feathersword, Dorothy the Dinosaur, and Wags the Dog.

Anthony with his surrogate family, his dogs.

The Day of the Teeth

I don't sleep a lot. Never have.

Maybe coming from a family of seven children and having spent six years at boarding school surrounded by hundreds of mischievous kids has got something to do with it. Or perhaps I got it from my father who loved nothing better than shaking us awake a few hours after we'd finished playing a late-night show with The Cockroaches.

I enjoy a peaceful snooze like anyone else, but there's something about being up before the birds that's invigorating. To this day I often get up around four in the morning. I don't feel like I can get everything done that needs to be done unless I'm roaming around the house as the sun comes up. Oh, and I still *love* good coffee—I take an espresso machine on the road with me everywhere. (America, with all due respect, you have to lift your coffee-game!)

Touring for 30 years plays havoc with your internal clock, particularly when you start popping pills to kill pain or drift off on a plane for a couple of hours sleep. But over the decades, I've generally found it relatively easy to slip into a routine of about five solid hours a night when I'm home and, for the most part, that's good enough. However, during that hectic period as we tried to break through in the U.S. and the U.K., I felt tired all the time. I remember for weeks at a time, I could barely lift my head off the pillow in the mornings. Even if I had a long night's sleep, I would lumber around the next day like the walking dead.

For the most part I ignored illness and injury. It was the exhaustion that most concerned me. I would raise the issue with medical professionals but they would inevitably redirect me to my obvious physical ailments—the back or neck pain, hernias, knee and ankle ligament strains and sprains—suggesting being tired was a by-product of the injury du jour. The variety of professionals I saw would do their best to diagnose and advise me accurately. But it was all so scattergun—they were patching my problems rather than solving them. Everyone seemed to understand what the issues were (I would have a new one every few weeks), but few, if any, could satisfactorily explain their root causes. Rather than treatment with a view to a cure, I came to expect advice and medication aimed at helping me merely cope with the situation.

And, in truth, at the time that's all I wanted. It was quick and easy. Sick of being exhausted, I'd try to change a few things, but in the end, I'd more or less give up (too exhausted to fight the exhaustion), figuring it was just the way it was going to be.

The prescribed pain killers didn't fix anything, but they stopped the hurt sometimes and helped me sleep. Of course, I realize now, that drug-induced "rest" helped create and nurture the fatigue rather than alleviate it, but at the time reaching for a pill seemed the only way to get through a tough period.

A potential light in my life was a romance I'd somehow managed to establish. She was a beautiful dancer with great talent, but unfortunately her international duties with the famed *Riverdance* franchise, combined with my overseas touring schedule, ensured we usually conducted the relationship from opposite sides of the world.

Absence may make the heart grow fonder, but on an extended basis it's a cruel barrier to allowing matters to flourish or die organically. It gave me another excuse to be grumpy and sad on the road. Dark clouds seemed to hover over my head too regularly, and it was a perfect storm of sorts that culminated in "the day of the teeth" in New York.

First, however, let me backtrack a bit. I mentioned earlier that I'd long had dental issues. I'd had slight tooth discoloration all my life and during my childhood I probably saw the dentist more than most kids. Most of it was minor work, or the result of my brothers trying to knock my teeth out, but things became far more precarious the older and more ill I got.

As I said earlier, I had become aware of the correlation between my emotional and physical health—one definitely impacting the other. Similarly, dental issues are like a barometer of overall health. But let's face it, you don't usually associate severe stomach pain with that toothache you're enduring. I certainly didn't until dental disaster struck me down.

I've learned that tooth decay often increases and gums become inflamed during periods of illness. Many conditions and medications decrease the flow of saliva in the mouth, undermining the strength of hard tissue (teeth) and swelling soft tissue (gums). Stress alone can lead to inflammation in the mouth inducing changes in the gums that some dentists believe are pre-cancerous.

Nevertheless for the most part, aching fangs and bleeding gums were well down on my list of "must fixes." And I barely ever gave a thought to the fact that my teeth were a little discolored because they had been from birth. But a film director we were working with suggested delicately that getting some of my teeth capped might be a fairly effortless cosmetic change that could be a positive, particularly as we geared up to take on America, where pearly whites are the rule not the sparkling exception.

So, a day or two prior to heading to the U.S. for a promotional tour, I booked an appointment to see a dentist in Sydney who insisted he had a fast and reliable method of capping teeth. I already was battling a round of ailments, and the extensive dental work made it even more difficult than usual to hop on the plane for the flight to New York. However I made it to the Big Apple in one piece courtesy of sleeping tablets and a thoughtful airline staff.

It was during my first meal out on the town—a piece of greasy but compelling New York pizza—that I found out that the "reliable" procedure was, in fact, quite flawed. I mean, a regular slice isn't good for you, I'll concede, but it's not supposed to dislodge half of the $7,000 dental job that had been done just two days prior. Yet there was the evidence, mixed with the tomato paste and tasty cheese, my caps, an odd topping if ever there was one. Not only was it upsetting and somewhat unattractive, it started to hurt like Hades.

Back at the hotel, I realized I needed to get to a dentist quickly. The gracious staff referred me to Dr. Jack, the hotel's regular emergency dentist in the city that never sleeps. He saw me promptly and recommended quick and comprehensive action. I wasn't going to argue, my mouth was on fire.

After he mentioned the work wouldn't be covered by insurance, Dr. Jack explained that he would have to extract multiple teeth. But he also had a revolutionary new capping system, basically consisting of two big multi-tooth caps—one for the top and one for the bottom. I was in the chair for two stretches of about ten hours each.

I was totally pain-pilled up, if there's such a term, so staggering through the streets of New York at various times of the day and night with my new shiny, pretend teeth and blood dribbling from my mouth are dreamlike flashbacks now. I think I killed the pain a little more during my stay in New York with a few pints, during several medicinal visits to Paddy Reilly's bar on the Lower East Side. This meant that the overnight calls to my dancer, somewhere else in the world, were even more incoherent than usual.

I paid the price on my return to Australia. My teeth continued to give me daily pain and I was swamped by stomach ailments, back spasms, neck stiffness, and intense headaches. Poor circulation had contributed to a serious varicose vein issue, for goodness' sake. I also was crippled by depression and in general despair about everything, especially the idea that I was letting The Wiggles down at a time when we needed to be at our peak.

Oh, and my love life? No pill or procedure has ever been invented to correct that issue. I could seek treatment for illness and injury but there was no cure for an empty heart. I was drained physically and emotionally, and my dancer, unfortunately though understandably, wasn't sympathetic.

The Cavalry Arrives

I needed help. There was no way I could keep running from it or putting it off. On a personal and professional basis I was completely overwhelmed. I could not dedicate enough time to my relationship and the beautiful dancer found it difficult to come to terms with the demands of my job. I was coming apart at the seams physically and our workload kept swelling as our international relationships became more complex.

What would have Dad done? Cracked a few jokes probably, before taking responsibility for the situation. If something's wrong, fix it. If you need help, ask for it. Put one foot in front of the other, and repeat.

My brother Paul had come on board in a managerial capacity with The Wiggles, helping to steady our ship. We had been a little too trusting of a few people as we pushed for international exposure and felt like things were running away from us. Even though our American partner, Lyrick, and the company's talented staff had been visionary, they had been taken over by a British company, Hit Entertainment and suddenly there was a chill in the air.

There was something odd about the British entertainment executives. They didn't get us at all and they weren't shy about letting us know. Ironically, we recruited our own Briton, Manchester boy Mike Conway, a friend of Greg Page's who also happened to be a leading corporate executive in Australia. Between Paul and Mike we felt the business of The Wiggles was in safe enough hands for us to look away occasionally. They knew our culture and understood what was important to us.

Even though Hit Entertainment seemed somewhat ambivalent, it was clearly time for us to commit to full scale, multi-month tours in the U.S. for the foreseeable future. If that was going to happen—if we were going to have to give it our best shot on our terms—I knew I had to get my affairs in order. But where to start?

I guess it was another light-bulb moment of sorts that put me on a path that, in retrospect, was the first positive move I'd made in a long time.

The First Step: Taking Responsibility

When you suffer from depression you often operate in an atmosphere that's clogged with self-doubt, self-loathing, and negativity. Fortunately I had professional help to guide me. Therapy was (and still is) a great way for me to make sense of my world, especially when it's being tarnished by negative thoughts or weighed down by the inertia of depression. I was prescribed, and used, an anti-depressant medication (sertraline hydrochloride) designed to impact the activity of a chemical, serotonin, in the brain. It helped from time to time, allowing me to stay in the moment and calming me when I needed it. But after a period—and in consultation with my doctor—I dispensed with it. Although I have few qualms about utilizing doctor-supervised medication again if required.

As I came to terms with the fact I was, and perhaps always will be, clinically depressed, I felt an urgent need to not only try and turn the ship around with professional help, but to come up with tools to steer myself out of trouble sometimes. I went looking for comfort and inspiration. I was raised a Catholic and had been surrounded by generations of my family who relished and embodied the compassionate spirit of the religion. Privately, I turned to prayer and became intrigued with the aspects of religious history. I'm particularly fond of the story of Our Lady of Guadalupe from sixteenth-century Mexico. No need to recount it here, but suffice it to say there are aspects of this beautiful tale that resonate with me—the victory of hope, belief, and compassion. I'm also enamored with the consistently magnificent effigies of Our Lady produced in Mexico and parts of the U.S.

Julio Iglesias, another of my musical heroes, probably had something to do with my growing fascination with the Spanish language cultures, too. He and Our Lady of Guadalupe are a formidable team. I'm not saying it was divine intervention, but making a spiritual connection helped me focus on the important things in life. Sharpening that vision was my frequent interaction with children, especially kids with special health issues.

Of all the fantastic opportunities The Wiggles experience has provided, the greatest of them is dealing regularly with sick or physically challenged children. Sometimes they'll attend our concerts and we'll have a chance for a meet and greet afterward, or on occasion—including every Christmas—I visit children's hospitals. Of course it's difficult not to be moved by their situation. In some cases pain is with them every minute, and their days are cluttered with therapies and tests. It's startling that they rarely complain, but what really takes my breath away is their ability to concentrate on the positive. Being exposed to that sort of character on a frequent basis is nothing short of awe inspiring.

I decided to shut the door on negativity. It pops open from time to time, but it's helpful if I close it quickly. Making that simple stand allowed me to get on with what I had to do. I couldn't wait for doctors and other experts to give me definitive answers about every aspect of my health but I could make a plan based on what I knew—that certain foods made me ill, that alcohol was often the elixir of depression, and that exercise was a way to shake away the gloom and improve my capacity to deal with illness and injury.

"I'm putting one foot in front of the other, Dad," I thought at the time.

First, the problem foods. I tried to formalize a process by which I could determine my food sensitivities. I gradually built a list of good and bad foods. Danger foods were plentiful. Doctors had already told me I had an allergy to tomatoes, but it was clear I was reacting to a crushingly wide variety of foods. I dropped most of the bad ones. Later, after extensive testing, medical specialists told me I had been wise to avoid nuts, chocolate, and wheat products, too. By systematically monitoring my intake I eventually arrived at an intricate understanding of not only what foods I should avoid completely, but others I needed to be cautious with.

I tried to avoid alcohol or at the very least keep track of how many drinks I had over a given period and record how each beverage impacted my mood and behavior. (Over the years I've come to terms with the fact that total abstinence is in my best interests, but I understand the desire to partake occasionally is stronger in some than others.)

My back pains and wonky knees made some exercise plans difficult to execute. Running, even walking more than a short distance, was out. Cycling seemed like a good idea, but I was so fragile psychologically that I had unreasonable fears (such as traveling over bridges!) that compromised that idea. Being surrounded by water in Sydney, swimming is a no-brainer, and it has the added advantage of being something you can do most anywhere in the world, particularly if you're overnighting, as I regularly do, in hotels.

I had no idea how to instigate an exercise plan based around swimming, but that's the glory of the activity; it's low impact and the simple act of doing it is helpful (to mind and body). I would trundle down to the delightful seawater pool near my home in Drummoyne in Sydney. At first, a few laps were more than enough, but by making a daily commitment and sticking to it, I improved rapidly.

Things began to click into place, I ate cautiously but heartily, exercised gently but regularly, and each night got the best five hours of sleep you could possibly wish for. Even on the road, at least for a while, I could support those habits.

3

Hope at Last

I was on track, for the first time in what felt like ages, but my personal life was still a sham. It had gotten to the stage where I truly believed it was impossible for me to continue to make the professional commitment required for The Wiggles to keep achieving their goals, and construct a private life to be shared with a special person. To be honest, after my dancer, I'd given up. Fortunately, though, my brother Paul—he who had done my bidding decades before—was cooking up a fiendishly brilliant scheme behind my back.

As The Wiggles boomed overseas, Paul's role expanded to be our eyes and voice on a bunch of issues, among them, reviewing artwork and other merchandising material. In that capacity he had frequent contact with a slender, elegant woman we'd both met in a professional context a few years before.

Michaela (Michelle or Miki) Patisteas used to work for legendary Australian merchandiser Fred Gaffney, who was closely associated with The Wiggles for many years. Paul and I had met

her at Dallas Brooks Hall in Melbourne. She was strikingly beautiful and refreshingly down to earth, but at the time, I was in a
relationship as was she, so that was that. However, as I slumped
into another lonely boy phase, Paul (I learned later), took it upon
himself to do a bit of a "hard-sell." He'd tell her that I had a nice
house and car and suggest that while I traveled a lot "you can
handle that." Gradually Paul let it slip he was doing my bidding
with "the beautiful Greek woman"—thereafter known as
TBGW—and he insisted she wasn't dismissing me out of hand.

My interest piqued, I decided to pay Michaela a visit in her
hometown of Melbourne, where her family owned the high-
profile gourmet brand, Griffith's Coffee. At the time Michaela had
moved on from Gaffney's and was working for her father, Peter, at
Griffiths, so I showed up at the factory saying that I wanted to buy
a coffee machine. It cost me a pretty penny, but not only did I get
a great coffee machine I got a tour of the factory from the owner's
charming daughter. Nevertheless, that looked like it for while,
because she was still feeling spent from a recent relationship. But
of course Paul would not be denied. Hearing that the end of her
relationship had left Michaela looking for a big change in her life,
my brother helped pave the way for her to secure a three-month
contract with a production company in my hometown of Sydney.

Believe me, despite my admiration for TBGW, the only female
I expected to see on most days for the rest of my life was Dorothy
the Dinosaur. The prospect of a romantic relationship was way
down on the list. Yet my brother persisted. One dinner date
couldn't hurt he said, and she is intelligent, funny, incredibly
attractive, and . . .

OK, OK, I'll Do It

I picked her up from her sister's place and headed to a pretty
little local Italian restaurant near my house in Hunters Hill in
Sydney. I was nervous, as usual, and I'd had a rather awkward

day—an acquaintance had been pestering me all day and was
spookily hanging around my home. And to be honest, I'm not
very good at dating, whatever that is. I'm a bit too restless to gaze
into someone's eyes over dinner (and I have a big appetite). I gib-
bered incoherently for the first part of the date but she was so
incredibly charming I just forgot myself. I had to enjoy this occasion to the max, I thought, so I ordered my favorite pasta dish.

Seems ignoring the tomato sensitivity even once in a blue
moon is not a good idea. I was soon doubled over with stomach
pain. Embarrassingly, I ended spending much of the *get to know
you* period in my own company in the restaurant bathroom.

If you could have seen the look on Michaela's sister's face
when I dropped her off before 9 p.m. Oh, the humiliation.

Yet, she apparently wanted to give it another go. I'm glad we
did, though I was full of dread. Not because I didn't care for her,
but because I had such a rotten relationship record and I didn't
want to subject myself or someone as lovely as Michaela to the
challenges of a long-distance romance.

But it blossomed. I guess it was pretty clear things were getting serious when I took Michaela to see Julio Iglesias perform. I
have very Catholic taste in music—I listen to a lot of different
genres—but there's something about Julio's cool, calculated Latin
groove that gets me every time.

Nevertheless, I wanted to proceed cautiously. After all, The
Wiggles' popularity was exploding in America and the band was
busy around the clock touring, recording, making new television
series, and developing videos.

Graceland

We hit the road, covering most major U.S. cities over several tours.
I tried to maintain some sort of health routine, swimming as often
as possible and staying away from the danger foods. It helped, but
I was experiencing horrendous headaches on a regular basis and

my gums and teeth were constantly sore. I remember being indignant. I was looking after myself like never before, but it seemed to have the net effect of giving me head pain.

At least the novelty of visiting new cities in North America helped make the traveling tolerable and the shows were fantastic. American audiences are so exuberant and willing to give you feedback during the performance.

I was particularly excited about one of the last stops on a lengthy tour—Memphis. Yes, Graceland. Finally I'd get a chance to visit Elvis Presley's home and resting place. The whole tour party was looking forward to that occasion. We even scheduled a full day off to be able to take it all in. The night before our planned visit, I was like a kid on Christmas Eve. A monster headache was spoiling things a little, but I'd learned to live with them. After a restless night's sleep, I tumbled out of bed at the first hint of dawn. "Elvis!" I thought. And then the pain grabbed me. It was excruciating. In my head, my mouth . . . everywhere. I was nauseated—I threw up—no help. I stumbled around looking for medication. I took something, who knows what.

Then the unthinkable happened. I had to shelve my plans to visit Graceland. As my friends and colleagues headed out for the day, I headed to the hospital. They took X-rays and a dental specialist was called in. I was told, in no uncertain terms, I needed extensive corrective dental work "right now." But the hospital was not in a position to perform the procedures I required: "We can't fix you, not sure who can," I remember a nurse saying. I needed a specialized dental surgeon, but I was 10,000 miles from home in a city where I knew no one. I made a snap decision to make the 30-hour trip back to Australia immediately. I called my mother in Sydney and asked her to set up treatment at her end for as soon as I arrived.

Loaded with painkillers, I made the journey from the hotel to the airport; the airport to dental surgery and on to a Sydney hospital. I can't remember much about the process except the look of horror on the dentist's face when he inspected my teeth. The work done months before in New York had been bad in the extreme. Teeth came out, titanium posts went in. Crowns and caps were replaced.

I was in the hospital for several days. When I came out I felt and looked like I'd been assaulted with a cricket bat which is much larger than a baseball bat. I headed home to rest, clutching pain killers. I couldn't figure out, at the time, why I needed at least four tablets to get some relief. Of course, much later I realized I'd been taking pills almost nightly for pain for a couple of years. No wonder one didn't work! Over a short period I had twenty-three root canal procedures. There wasn't a day for the better part of a year when I didn't have some dental pain.

There's a scene in one of our DVDs, *Wiggle Bay*, which was shot in 2002, where we are all romping in the surf and you'll notice I'm doing a very peculiar dance. I remember it vividly. I got a mouthful or two of sea water, one of the great natural medicinal agents. It was attacking my ongoing gum infections and sensitive teeth and probably doing me a load of good, but it was hellishly painful. I was literally hopping about moaning.

I took comfort in my religious ponderings and the fact that I had a wonderful relationship with Miki who wasn't afraid to tell me to "man up" when the pain was extreme. I headed to Mexico during one trip to North America and in a moment of madness got a very large tattoo on my upper arm (which I hid from fans for a long time) of Our Lady of Guadalupe. My mother's classic quote when she first saw it: "Anthony Field, it took me nine months to produce that arm and about an hour for you to destroy it." Interestingly, when I got the tattoo, an elaborate, detailed illustration, I was so hopped up on pain killers, I didn't to feel a thing—I actually fell asleep in the tattooist's chair.

The Full Imprimatur

By the end of 2002 we knew we were involved in something extraordinary in the U.S. A few little television spots on the Disney

Channel got incredible ratings reactions, leading to the cable network screening our Australian-made television series. Despite the modest production values of the old programs, they caught on with preschoolers. Our concert schedule in North America doubled, seemingly overnight, and there was talk of people paying $500 for tickets—not something we encourage, but a fascinating gauge of the high level of interest.

On a personal level, I was basking in the glow of my relationship with Miki and trying to keep a variety of ailments at bay. I was getting better at maintaining some sort of health routine on the road and identifying potential food afflictions, although I'd slip up from time to time. On one long haul flight, I'd nibbled something that apparently contained nuts. Even though they were on my list of *no-nos*, nuts hadn't caused me any great distress before. However the resulting stint in the business class lavatory was embarrassing in the extreme. I literally couldn't get out of there for most of the trip. Eventually the poor flight attendants resorted to giving me charcoal tablets, a natural remedy for many stomach ailments. Unfortunately, charcoal tablets had never encountered a digestive system quite like mine.

Nevertheless I somehow managed to make it across oceans and continents to meet our obligations and enjoy the chance to play to hundreds of thousands of preschool children. The travel filled me with dread, for more than one reason, but I always knew I would see Miki on return, a prospect that filled me with unreasonable joy and contentment. But I still had cold feet and didn't really allow myself to think too much about the possibility of her being my partner for life. In fact, to my shame, I hadn't even told her I loved her.

Before one tour departure, I called my dear aunty, my dad's sister, Marie Truman, who was stricken with cancer and quite possibly unlikely to be around on my return. Aunty Mar had met Miki and commented that she had "my full imprimatur." On the way to the airport I turned her comment over in my head, again and

again. It was the same phrase my father had always used—giving
his imprimatur to anything was the ultimate endorsement. Suddenly, after months of avoiding the inevitable by admitting I was
head over heels in love, I came to my senses. "What am I doing?" I
thought. "I love this woman and I'm just stringing her along." Right
then and there I rang Miki and proposed over the phone. It was a
pretty bad line, but I think she accepted. (I did the *formal* deed,
getting down on one knee, on my return from the tour.)

We'd have to squeeze in the wedding in between tours. Life
was more hectic than ever, but The Wiggles were on top of the
world and I had finally found the kind of relationship my parents
had enjoyed. I swam regularly, trying to keep the weight off and
keep illness at bay for the big day. Generally speaking, I was successful and, accordingly, my psychological state was relatively har-
monious.

During the week before the wedding, in May 2003, I had been
scrambling to complete a few Wiggles tasks. Despite my best
efforts to stay on top of things, I'd been slowed down somewhat
by sickness; the usual stuff, headache, nausea, tiredness. But there
was so much to do professionally and personally that I pushed it
to the back of my mind as I raced through Sydney's suburban
streets in my car from appointment to appointment. Driving
through traffic I became aware of something not being right. I
don't know exactly what happened, but the thing I remember is
waking up on the side of the road, the car still running.

I had fainted. Somehow, fortunately, I'd managed to pull over
before doing so. It was a frightening experience, but I tried to
dismiss it as a symptom of being nervous about the countdown to
the big day.

The wedding was a blast. Miki looked ravishing in a traditional
white gown made by The Wiggles' wardrobe designer, Maria
Petrozzi (mother of my chiropractor mate Johnny), while I went
for a different look in a mariachi suit, sans sombrero, much to my
mother's relief.

Anthony and Miki on their wedding day

We planned a honeymoon in the Greek Islands—we still haven't got around to it. Touring commitments cluttered my calendar immediately after the wedding and for the following eight years or so. The important thing was, I'd done the deed and it was oh, so right! I can't remember ever being happier.

And then, a week later, I collapsed.

Waking in the hospital my first coherent thought was "not now." Just as everything was finally coming together, I'd gone and fallen in a heap. In fact, this was no isolated collapse. Things were serious—very serious. The infections from the clumsy dental work I'd had years before had never really left me. They'd seeped into my nasal cartilage and skull. Guess that explained some of the headaches. Doctors performed urgent surgery to scrape the bone clean of the infection and I was bombed with medications to clean up the problem and prevent it from coming back, although there were no guarantees. I was told I was lucky to be alive. A few more weeks or even days without attention and perhaps I wouldn't have been.

I'd been scared before, but not like this. I had so much to live for. My beautiful wife was pregnant! I vowed to make a supreme effort to get my health back, but I would have to do it on the road. For the most part, I stuck to that promise, but the first domino had fallen and the flow-on was inevitable. While Miki endured a difficult pregnancy in our first year of marriage, I lurched from illness to illness. I had circulation problems that put me into the hospital and contributed to my varicose vein issue (which required surgery) and I was struck down by a double hernia.

I got further specialist advice about my digestive system. I had colitis (inflammation of the colon) and irritable bowel syndrome symptoms. My bad foods list expanded ... and expanded.

After one six-week long tour, I arrived back in Sydney, relieved to be in one piece and anxious to see Miki. I headed straight for the little cafe we had purchased in inner Sydney where she was working the coffee machine. Despite aggravating my chronic back injury on the road I was bursting with anticipation until I got in the door and something I had eaten on the plane took issue with me. What a homecoming. I spent two hours in the lavatory out back and when I finally emerged, my back was aching so much I was hunched over.

This was no way to live. I had tried to turn things around but had failed. I wasn't going to give up, but it was time to shake things up completely. I had to change my lifestyle, maybe even change my career.

Baby Makes Three

Marriage, I'm assured, is good for your health. Unfortunately, I didn't get the memo. Not in that first year, anyway. Poor Miki. What must she have thought as I spent most of the first twelve months of our union either in the hospital, at home sick in bed, or on the road? However, at times, I was happier than I'd ever been. I reveled in the chance to create a new life with my wife. We had a new home and wasted no time building a family.

Lucia Maria Angela Field was born on February 2, 2004, a 7 lb (3.175 kg) dark-haired beauty like her mother. I got to spend just about every waking moment with my new child in the first few months of her life, but then it was back on the road. The Wiggles were booming in North America. Our television program was rating its socks off and we couldn't accommodate the demand for tickets to our concerts. We almost doubled our touring commitment in order to get to the major cities.

Contentment at home, I'm afraid, didn't transfer to our time on the road. In fact knowing Miki and Lucia were an ocean and continent away made touring even more agonizing. Fortunately, with Miki's support, I had developed healthier eating habits, but chronic back and neck pain plagued me and was exacerbated by the dancing in our shows.

I had all but given up visiting medical general practitioners. One of my main complaints continued to be fatigue, but I was reminded by several doctors in several countries that moving between time zones and maintaining my schedule would make me weary. In Australia, I had been told I was suffering from fibro-myalgia and one medical specialist advocated I undergo testing to examine the possibility I was also dealing with something I'd never heard of before—chronic fatigue syndrome.

I wanted to be able to give things "a name" but I was too busy coping with pain and trying to remain upright long enough to do what I had to do, to spend time establishing I had *another* thing for which to take medication.

The only relief I seemed to get was from chiropractors. My buddy in Australia, Johnny Petrozzi, had eventually talked me into allowing him to give me adjustments. Previously I'd been a skeptic, but unquestionably a single visit to the chiropractor pro-vided more relief than countless other exercises and treatments I'd tried. Johnny would patch me up, wag his finger at me for using pain medication, and send me out on the road.

Unfortunately, once I was out there, things usually fell apart quickly. Our backstage masseurs would try to get me mobile, but nothing would work. Eventually, I developed a little routine—the first thing I'd do after arriving in a small town or city was to track down a local chiropractor.

The penny dropped. Why not replace the masseurs with chi-ropractors? The impact was immediate. The health of the entire Wiggles cast and crew improved virtually overnight and it helped me immeasurably. I have no doubt I would have been unable to perform at least half of our scheduled concerts in 2003 and 2004 had it not been for the chiropractors we picked up in different regions of North America.

Nevertheless, I still struggled mightily at times, spending nights on hardwood floors in hotels to alleviate back pain and standing for hours during the day, afraid to sit down for fear of not being able to get back up again. Months on the road felt like years as we curtailed our extracurricular activities just so we could make it to the stage. For the most part, I'd spend concert days either performing or being adjusted on the chiropractor's table. We couldn't risk doing much else. Even our plastic bat and ball cricket games—the equivalent of stickball—played backstage in some of the great concert venues in Australia and North America had to be cut. It wasn't just me. Pagey, the youngest in the group (and an excellent pace bowler with a high action), had to give it up, as chronic injuries, made worse by the physicality of our show, took their toll.

Enough!

I decided I had to change something, as the glorious early stages of my marriage were punctuated by bouts of illness and extreme pain. At the back of my mind, I played with the idea of getting off the road for good, perhaps reinventing The Wiggles or simply replacing the Blue Wiggle on stage. Yet, I lived to be able to perform for young kids. Our show was getting better and better and I really felt like we had so much more to give.

After about four months straight on the road, however, I was done—burned like blackened toast. My general health was so bad I couldn't even exercise. I was eating empty calories and putting on weight again.

The dark cloud was following me. Miki had rarely seen me consumed by depression—I could hide it somewhat by being on the road—but my poor Wiggles colleagues witnessed me on more than one occasion, inexplicably bawling my eyes out in the dressing room.

It wasn't fair to anyone.

My chronic pains were more intense than ever. I was tired all the time, felt like I had a cold I couldn't shake, and endured awful headaches. One day while on tour in Chicago, I took a walk along the shore of Lake Michigan. Who was I fooling? I'd had enough; I really didn't think I could carry on with The Wiggles. I called Miki and told her I was at the end with my touring career. I was sick and miserable as hell and just couldn't see myself doing it well into the future. But there was a tour to complete. The Chicago shows had been sold out, and the fact that I really loved that town helped spur me on. The immediate problem, however, had nothing to do with quitting—it was how I was going to get myself back on stage. My back and hip were aching as never before. I could barely walk, let alone dance.

As always, we'd hired a local chiropractor to help us out backstage. Before our first show I introduced myself to Doctor James Stoxen and requested an adjustment to help me get through the shows. After a quick chat, Dr. Stoxen, who has a big reputation in the showbiz world, indicated he would be able to help, but insisted on giving me a full examination. He said I had substantial health issues that were quite apparent to him and needed to be addressed. He tried to be delicate, but he let me know he could detect I was on the verge of some sort of physical collapse. As much as I appreciated his concern, I was more focused on just getting through the performances. I would work out the "big" issues later. Besides, all I wanted to do was get back to my family. I would crawl back to them if necessary.

"Come on, Doc," I thought to myself at the time. "Who's paying for this? I've got a show to do, just give me the adjustment and we can discuss all this other stuff another time." I can be quite demonstrative, particularly when it comes to my work, and I remember pointedly remarking that I had a lot to do before the show, so could we get on with it.

In retrospect, I believe I could probably detect that Dr. Stoxen was on to something. It was both exhilarating and a little frightening. I hate to admit it, but sometimes when you're ill or injured, it almost feels like it's easier to accommodate the handicap rather than face the challenge of eliminating it. As real as it is, pain becomes a habit that's hard to break. It's caused so much disruption in my life that I've had to embrace it in order to simply cope.

And then there are the scars from the times when I have tried and inevitably failed to change things. The will to be healthy is as important as any physical intervention. I had all but lost that desire.

The Diagnosis

I was shuffling about, looking for an excuse to limp out of the room when the doctor said something that hit home: "You've taken ownership of your injuries and illnesses, haven't you? I bet you remember the day you got that herniated disc or shin splint." Remember? I could have told him the exact dates.

You say to yourself: "I used to be able to do this before this injury and that before that injury." It's like life is broken down into before and afters.

"Well, it's time to make a new date to remember—the day when you started to get better." Hmm, this guy wasn't into band-aid treatments, it would seem. I sat down. "Do your worst," I thought. After all, I was convinced I'd seen it all before.

"Take your shoes and socks off," he said. My shoes and socks? It was my back hurting, not my toes.

"Your shoes and socks."

When I complied, he explained that he'd watched me walk around backstage, and from my gait could tell right away that I had serious problems.

"But it's my back!" I protested as I walked around in bare feet.

"What about the pain in your right knee, right foot, and right hip?" he responded. Amazingly, he could tell just from watching me walk, precisely where I was experiencing pain. *Next he'll be telling me about the headaches I'd been having.* "And about those regular headaches of yours?"

Now just hang on a second. I'd seen so many doctors in my life and paid so much money to have problems unsuccessfully evaluated and treated, they should have named a hospital wing after me, and this guy watches me walk for three minutes and knows my life story?

"You've got chronic arthritis," Dr. Stoxen continued, "from toe to head."

Chronic arthritis? My grandfather had that just before he died! Come on, I might be considered old for a guy who jumps around on stage singing kids' songs, but not *that* old. And, oh, by the way, what have my feet got to do with it? "Your human spring has broken down because of a weakness in the pronator-supinator cuff muscles supporting the arch of your foot," the doctor said. "You're all locked up. The spring mechanism that runs through you body is jammed."

Of course! My spring mechanism and the old pronator-super . . . what???

"The spring suspension system muscles of your pelvis are weak too and that's why you have chronic lower back pain." My look of complete confusion didn't go unnoticed. The doctor explained that his method of evaluation and treatment is based on the concept that the human body is, in a sense, a giant spring— "from toe to head," he said.

The spring suspension system is the interconnected mechanism that basically governs and protects the way we move. He said he coined the term "pronation-supination cuff muscles" to refer to the muscles strategically attached to the undersurface of foot arches to facilitate the "spring" as you walk.

"In the course of a year, your feet will hit the ground in motion about 3.6 million times," he said. "That's from walking, running, and in your case dancing. It adds up to 100 million collisions over thirty years. It's quite an impact. And that's the first of the three main functions of the human spring mechanism—to protect you in that process."

When your foot lands, the suspension muscles control the lowering of the arch of the foot and support other weight-bearing joints, allowing your body weight to be absorbed gradually. This, he explained, produces a softer landing and reduces shock to the skeleton. When those suspension muscles are weak, the support is diminished, specifically in the arch of the foot. Gradually, the spring deteriorates and the arch spring locks, meaning when you walk, every step produces a "bang and twist" impact leading to stress and strain in every joint in the body.

"This abnormal motion keeps the joints in a constant stress and a strained state which, not only produces pain, but challenges the body's natural ability to heal itself," he said.

Maybe that was a reason I could never shake aches and pains.

Second, the spring mechanism is the way the body recycles energy. The doctor grabbed an old mattress spring from his bag—clearly he'd done this before. "When you step down, the weight of your body deforms the arch shape and loads weight into the human spring like what happens when you squeeze any spring down—it loads energy and stores it.

"This stored energy is released as your foot leaves the ground. Boiing!"

The recycling process is impeded should the spring supports or any of the joints in the foot or ankle (there's 33 of them) be weak or locked. Finally the human spring, when functioning correctly, allows us to move normally: "The way our moving parts were designed and engineered to move," he said. "Stress free and that's the key to avoiding constant joint degeneration also known as chronic arthritis." The arthritis thing again. OK, OK I get it.

The bottom line is if your spring system is a mess, it's like trying to drive a car without any suspension. It's not just a bumpy ride—fairly swiftly the vehicle will literally start to fall apart.

"The body has to work harder to do simple motoring tasks instead of utilizing free, recycled spring energy," he explained. Accordingly, this is why millions of people are trapped in a cycle of chronic fatigue and pain. "And all that hard work is tiring, exhausting in the extreme" leading, Dr. Stoxen believes, to widespread misdiagnosis for such conditions as chronic fatigue syndrome and fibromyalgia. I was in constant pain, diagnosed with fibromy-algia and displaying symptoms of chronic fatigue. I could relate.

Apparently, my pronator-super-doopers were duds and my human spring, was, well, sprung. After years of dead ends, I felt I'd finally hit on something that was making sense. Cause and effect—possibly there were reasons why I was like this after all. It wasn't just a bunch of mystery afflictions I was neither able to track or treat.

The doctor explained that a lack of appropriate exercise, and my weight increase, had taken their toll. The muscles had been weakened, meaning, instead of helping the arch spring back as I walked, my foot was rolling inward, sparking a biomechanical meltdown of sorts that impacted my legs, hips, and back.

"Your arches have collapsed inward, so your knees and thighs torque inward," Dr. Stoxen explained. "Every step is causing stress and strain—on every joint in your body." And I thought the arches of my feet were one of my better features. "Look," I said as I pointed to them, "they're high. They look like the Sydney Harbor Bridge."

But the doctor put an end to that line of thought. Height isn't the issue—"The spring's the thing," he preached. You can have arches as flat as the Nullabor Plain, but if the pronator-supinators are working properly, you'll have bounce and balance in every step.

No More Shortcuts

A memorable feature of that first interaction with Doc James was the fact that he explained everything to me. I went back to him later to gain an intricate understanding of his method, which we'll explore in detail later in this book. But even during the initial consultation he provided enough information to help me connect a bunch of dots about my health situation that convinced me there was hope. That was a rare experience. It was such a contrast to most of the medical consultations I'd had over the years. I, like you, no doubt, had endured doctor after doctor silently inspecting me and summarily dismissing me, perhaps scribbling a prescription to tide me over.

It might sound like a funny parallel, but in some way I equated the way many professionals treat their patients with the way some traditional children's performers treat their audiences. The Wiggles had deliberately worked to change that oftentimes condescending relationship, by empowering children at our shows, being direct and inclusive, and encouraging curiosity and enthusiasm. We want them to go home informed, entertained, and feeling the desire to learn more about the world around them.

I felt a similar charge during my time with Dr. Stoxen. I was a participant in what was going on, not merely an observer or, in some cases, victim. He put it to me: "I'll treat you but you have to be willing to put in the work too. You have to be motivated to change this." To find that motivation he asked me to think about a couple of things. First, to be fearful of what might happen if I didn't act and, conversely, consider what great things might happen if I did.

After stints in the hospital and a brush with death I didn't have to work too hard to picture how bad things could become, although the doctor helped fire up the imagery with a few statistics and other facts about back surgeries, osteoporosis, and knee and hip replacements. Joint replacement surgeries are almost standard practice in the U.S., U.K., and Australian health systems. About 400,000 a year are performed in the U.S. alone, that's 4 million or so in the last ten years.

"It's not just the surgeries, it's the rehab. It hurts," he reminded me.

Maybe worse is the fact that many thousands of replacement surgeries have to be repeated or corrected. And then there's the chance of infection and vulnerability to additional injury because of one's frail state. Even if I avoided surgery my mobility would likely be restricted by arthritis pain, diagnosed in as many as seventy million Americans. And fibromyalgia, a condition blamed for debilitating about four million Americans, was booming in Canada, the U.K., and Australia. I also was a prime candidate for obesity, especially if I stopped exercising or performing. After twenty-five years of chronic joint pain, the prospect of me motoring about in one of those electric wheelchairs in a decade or so was looking very real.

"Now think about what will happen if you take these challenges on and defeat them," the doctor said.

That wasn't hard either. I immediately thought of my daughter. Eventually she would be racing around the yard in Sydney, perhaps with brothers and sisters and her (maybe) healthy father in tow. My kids could have a childhood like mine, close to the bosom of a family, steered by parents who lived life to the fullest—entertaining, laughing, singing, loving, and caring. They could have a father like mine, seemingly indestructible and able to do anything.

I pictured Miki at the end of a tour, welcoming me—not having to help me into the car or offering a shoulder to lean on so I could stagger to bed to lie down. I saw myself rising gleefully and healthfully at 4 a.m. peeking out at the quiet, dark beauty of the waters of Sydney Harbor, a cup of strong coffee in hand, and the prospect of a day of creative challenges ahead. I thought of the beaming faces of the kids in the crowd at Wiggles concerts. The wondrous sight of children laughing, dancing, and singing while being embraced by their moms and dads. No one with a care and no one with a worry.

And I thought about the sick and handicapped children I'd met over the years. Some of them had gone now, battlers to the end—their smiles, despite the pain, and their excitement at meeting The Wiggles. What a gift.

"I'm in, Doc," I said. "Let's do this." It was August 14, 2004. My new date to remember.

Stepping in the Right Direction

It's a little scary to know that some of the children who came to our shows when we first started The Wiggles have kids themselves now. We've actually employed people in recent years to perform as our costume characters—Dorothy the Dinosaur, Wags the Dog, and Henry the Octopus—who got to know us when they were very young children, watching our videos and dancing at our shows. It makes you feel, er, wise (and maybe a little old).

It's satisfying, in a sense, to realize we've stood the test of time and managed, to a degree, to move with the times. Though frankly, while we've sought to improve what we do over the years, our focus has always been pretty much the same. We concentrate on making what we do developmentally appropriate and fun. That's the golden rule. We look for different ways to do it every so often, but a primary goal, as always, is to let kids be kids. And not much has changed in terms of our audience of preschoolers.

Whether it's 1991 three-year-olds or 2012 toddlers, all react positively to being allowed, encouraged, and empowered to be curious, learn, and enjoy themselves. The most notable things to change have been the haircuts and the clothes, although the old styles seem to be swinging around again. We've noticed too the rise in the number of children who might have issues with their weight (about a third of children in the U.S. are obese or over-weight, with similar figures in Australia), and definitely, we meet more children on the autism spectrum.

That observation is supported by statistics. In the United States it is estimated 1 in 114 children (and as many as 1 in 67 in one study) are on the spectrum, an umbrella term for a wide range of psychological conditions including Asperger's syndrome. That percentage has grown rapidly in recent decades, and the number of children diagnosed continues to rise at a rate of up to 17 percent per year. Similar figures in Australia, Great Britain, and elsewhere point to a health crisis that is exploding.

It is another reminder for me of how fortunate I am to be able to do what I do with The Wiggles. Obviously we don't have answers to complex issues, but we can provide an outlet, an opportunity to bring families together in the simple quest to be entertained and, as a community, celebrate our kids, many of whom face these incredible challenges. What's remarkable is not how different children, as a group, are from state to state, country to country, but how similar. And that hasn't changed much over the years.

A fantastic experience is encountering children in the street, be it in New York, Sydney, London, Dublin, Hong Kong, Singapore, Beijing, or Taipei. Sometimes it's a relief when they don't recognize me, for example, when I'm trying to wrangle my own kids (no Wiggles blue shirt or belt buckle helps in that regard). For the most part, though, they'll just wander up and tell me what's on their mind: "You're the Blue Wiggle," or they ask about Wags or Dorothy or maybe let me know "Captain Feathersword is funny." Then they move on.

But among my favorite encounters are those with the little ones who stop suddenly in their tracks in the street and stare. It happens a lot and they're usually standing about three feet in front of me. They've gotten close enough to recognize me and freeze—or they know my face but are trying to process why I haven't got my stage costume on. It's like a stand-off. They don't move an inch and I feel obliged to stay where I am while they work things out. Some of these episodes end with the children just walking away, maybe keeping a watchful eye on me but saying nothing.

Among the parents, our American friends are usually incredibly enthusiastic and complimentary. In Australia, we are kind of part of the furniture and the Aussie culture is typically laconic, so it's usually a nod, a "g'day," and maybe a quip about the absence of the blue shirt.

Recently I was shopping near my home in Sydney. I was at my glamorous best, wearing trackie dacks (long track pants in American parlance), a West Tigers rugby league jersey (go Tigers), and a big cap. When I got to the checkout counter the cashier did a double take.

"You look like that guy from The Wiggles," she suggested. "You really do!"

OK, I thought, busted. But before I could flash my best Wiggle smile she said "Nah, you're not him, but I bet you wish you had his money."

"Yeah," I said. "That would be great."

When we get to have conversations with parents about their children and The Wiggles it's surprising how many people ask the same questions or make the same observations. Sometimes it's "you must really love being on tour . . . all that travel"—I can only smile in response to that one. Oftentimes, though, I'm asked what I love best about what I do.

That's a tough question to answer as well, in so far as where do I start? It's kind of my life-blood. God knows what would have

Anthony with John Travolta.

happened to me if I'd bowed out of performing back in 2004. And that is probably the answer—the show. It's what I love doing most; making the show better and better.

The buzz of meeting the challenge of constructively communicating with children in an ultra-positive environment is fantastic but the entire experience is a blessing. Even before we go on stage, there are precious moments listening to the audience getting prepared for the big show. The pre-show routine and the opening vary from year to year, place to place, but quite often we use a recorded overture as a warm-up.

As the house lights ease down and the overture comes up, the twitter of excitement in the auditorium becomes a buzz of expectation punctuated by the toddlers' ecstatic squeals. The overture, a compilation of Wiggles songs, gets the kids moving . . . Toot Toot, Hot Potato, Fruit Salad. . . .

Inevitably, as the first few recorded bars of our song "Rock-a-Bye Your Bear" roll out of the speakers, you hear thousands of mothers (and some of the dads) in the audience form a spontaneous chorus. Taking a peek from behind the curtain I see them gently squeezing their little ones with delight and urging them to join in.

Everybody clap. Everybody sing.

La-la-la-la-la!

Bow to your partner. Then you turn around.

Yippee!

Hands in the air, rock-a-bye your bear.

Bear's now asleep . . . ssh-ssh-ssh.

And at that moment, everything is right with the world. You can feel it like a cooling, cleansing breeze on a torridly hot day. The problems of everyday life and the thought of issues, afflictions, and horrors that mums, dads and kids may have to confront in the future—pimples, girls, boys, drugs, sports, jobs, cars, violence, careers, talk-back radio—all of them gone, gone. The globe briefly, unarguably, is a glorious place. Our children are safe and immeasurably happy.

When the overture swells to a crescendo and seconds later we race onto the stage waving and smiling, the excitement bubbles over. Parents and kids wave back like we're making a welcome return to their lives. Few things are more gratifying.

Our first show was at a friend's daycare facility in Randwick, in Sydney, in 1991, for about a dozen kids. It was rudimentary to say the least and the production values didn't change much for quite a few years. It was just us four guys doing funny little dances we thought the kids could emulate and singing pop songs about issues they could relate to.

Of course it grew into a major production, although our dancing didn't improve much! Luckily we surrounded ourselves with talented people both on and off stage who helped add a WOW factor to the experience.

By 2004 we were hauling about sixty people around North America, using several equipment trucks and a couple of tour buses. Fortunately Fatty didn't insist on driving.

Most of the venues we played from coast to coast were 3,000 seats or more (sometimes 10,000 in the larger cities) and we'd often play two to three concerts a day over the course of a few days in each location. In New York in 2003 we sold out Madison Square Garden for a record twelve straight shows.

In Chicago, that's what I'd been contemplating turning my back on—the show, the people, and the places. I can't tell you what a relief it was emerging from that weekend of treatment knowing that I wouldn't have to take myself off the road. I wouldn't have to pull the plug on the cast and crew and the opportunities for those precious encounters with kids.

PART TWO

My Health Journey

4

The Human Spring 101

The Purple Wiggle, Mr. Jeffrey Fatt, hatched a plan a few decades ago to record his adventurous life. Every day from January 1, 1990, Fatty has taken at least one photograph, usually of the people he's spending time with that day. Thus his visual diary has hundreds of shots of his bandmates, hardly any flattering— many downright bizarre. Scrolling through the snapshots, it is fun trying to remember what you were doing on that particular day and what was going on at the time. It's hard to get the details right—it's disturbing how much you forget over the decades.

But there are a couple of things consistently notable: Fatty has barely aged despite being as old as Methuselah, Murray's hair is really red, and I've had more "looks" than Madonna (though none of them featured skimpy skirts, or fishnet stockings). Strangely when I glance at the photos I can't remember, for the most part, what was going on in my life at that moment, but I can tell you what illness I was coping with. It's ridiculous!

There are a few photos of me that conjure up sickly memories—I look like death, with the blank stare I always associate with episodes of depression. And I'm slightly disheveled, as if I'd been sleeping in the clothes I'm wearing that day.

While it's difficult to recall where most of the photos were taken, a few places we visit regularly seem to stand out. One of them, Chicago, has provided us with some great experiences over the years and that's reflected in Fatty's diary. The Sears Tower, the House of Blues, and the Hancock Observatory. It's a great livable town—kind of like Melbourne on steroids. We've visited every year since about 2000 and rarely do Chicago and its people disappoint or fail to surprise. From our eating expeditions (I love the Italian sandwiches, though I'm not supposed to eat them!) to the city's great music scene. It's a sports town and a place that invites exploration, despite the blustery wind and cold. Recently I charged down the Navy Pier on my fold-up bicycle—there were a bunch of other bikes around so I felt part of the community—until a couple of angry officials told me I had gate-crashed a race. Most of the locals in the race just laughed it off.

Back in 2004, the surprise was coming into contact with Dr. Stoxen. I hadn't expected to make a sudden commitment to a new treatment approach minutes before taking the stage at the Allstate Arena in the Windy City, but that town had ambushed me again. Even though the doctor had provided me with a glimmer of hope, I wasn't necessarily entertaining the idea of a sudden and significant turnaround, so I was still thinking that those shows would be among my last. I was hobbled. I couldn't sit down for more than a few minutes because my back would freeze up. Even if I hauled myself up, my knees would buckle and my feet ached. (I could hear a click every time I took a step, but I never really worked out where it was coming from.)

I didn't get to indulge in the charms of Chicago on that visit. Over the course of a weekend, I spent all my time either onstage, on the treatment table backstage, or flat on my back getting treated in my hotel room.

It's not the way other healers do business but it was clear to Dr. Stoxen that I needed constant treatment if I was going to get through a weekend of shows. For three to five hours at a time he'd work on me. It was grueling, but I didn't know what the future held, so I couldn't let that opportunity slip.

Subsequently we condensed several weeks of treatment into a few days. Dr. Stoxen has a precise and considered touch, but trying to do so much in such little time meant a few of the procedures hurt. Though the most noticeable physical reaction is actually feeling energy and blood flowing through your body, rejuvenating and refueling muscles, limbs, and joints—we called it pain exorcism.

Those first sessions were almost comical in one respect. Right up until the moment I ran onstage, he was working on me furiously. When there was a few minutes' break in the show, I would charge backstage for treatment, then, immediately post-show, we were back at it.

I learned a lot about my body—the human body in general—my issues and what could be done about them from Dr. Stoxen's running commentary that weekend, which I'll recount in coming pages. As it became evident his approach was something vastly different from the usual diagnose/treatment model, I was curious to know how he formulated his ideas and developed his method.

That is, Doc, tell us where in the name of chronic pain did all this stuff come from?

Plyometrics

The son of a chiropractor, Dr. Stoxen decided early in his career to not only specialize in spinal care, but to develop the knowledge and expertise to train champion athletes. In the course of his work he became fascinated with narrowing down the specific physical reasons why some people, for example, can run marathons while others struggle to walk around the block. He wanted to know exactly what was going on in the body when we move—in essence, the secrets to improving human performance.

Frequently working with athletes in the late 1980s he was struck by an apparent disconnect between the way coaches trained their charges—often via high-impact drills—and the prevailing wisdom in the medical community, which largely frowned on such "risky" practices, insisting frequent running and jumping routines would swiftly lead to degeneration of the joints. "There was so much conflicting information and advice, on both sides," he said. "When I broke it down, it was pretty clear to me many decisions were being shaped by a general misunderstanding of human mechanics."

Many of the modern high-impact training methods gained favor first in the old Soviet Union where the Dr. Stoxen was a regular visitor and an official team doctor for a number of U.S. national sports team.

The Soviets dominated speed and power sports for a couple of decades. While there is ongoing suspicion about the use of performance-enhancing drugs in some disciplines during that period, it was clear at the time and even more evident in retrospect that their innovative training methods were far and away more advanced than those commonly employed in the west.

American coaches and trainers had tried to incorporate some of those techniques but a lack of easy communication between the U.S. and Soviet experts during those cold war years meant not all coaches were fully briefed in the new methods. As a result, during this time of experimentation, some athletes were put at risk. Applying the new high-impact training methods without having an intricate understanding of what they were doing to the body resulted in some needless injuries, which played into the traditional medical community's assertion that such approaches should be avoided.

But Dr. Stoxen, who we've established is rather difficult to dissuade, had seen, firsthand, the potential of some of the techniques employed in the mysterious Soviet Union. So around the time I was eating too much in Chinese restaurants and jumping around onstage in remote parts of Australia with The Cockroaches, he was investigating the ideas and evaluating the discoveries made by the man considered to be one of the founders of these training methods. The late Dr. Yuri Verhoshansky is widely acknowledged as the "father" of plyometrics. Plyometrics is an approach to training that seeks to bolster explosive power, by conditioning muscles to contract with an uncommon intensity and aid the body's ability to recoil elastically.

"It's human spring training," Dr. Stoxen said.

The high-impact training drills employed in plyometrics enhance the effect of traditional resistance exercises. They develop and tune the components of the human spring, helping to better recycle energy through the body and prevent injury by providing a buffer between joints while encouraging stress- and strain-free motion.

There is a little debate about the worth and safety of plyometrics throughout the sports world these days (it is used in most every form of elite training—something we'll explore a little later), but as it slowly emerged from behind the old Iron Curtain it was met with suspicion.

For Dr. Stoxen, however, it reinforced much of what he already knew and pointed him in a direction to develop treatment and training techniques not only to take athletes to the next level but to uncover reasons why those of us at the other end of the scale—the limping "everyman" with chronic injuries—are buried in the maze of daily pain and debilitation.

Employing large doses of logic, he concluded that if a stronger human spring results in improved overall strength, speed, and balance then a weakened mechanism will have the opposite effect, such as reduced performance levels, loss of balance, poor coordination, and less agility and strength.

"It's so obvious," Dr. Stoxen said. "I needed to explore the concept that if spring strength is the secret to optimum performance then the loss of the human spring is behind the decline of health. Also, spring and elasticity is part of youthfulness, while the loss of that is what we encounter in aging, so if we can restore the spring, do we slow the aging process?

"Oh yes we do. Yes we do!"

A New Way of Looking

There are several reasons why I'm a children's entertainer and not a doctor. One is that patients would look at me strangely if I started to sing and dance midconsultation. And of course there is the little matter of years of medical study and training.

The rush of information from Dr. Stoxen when I first met him was pretty overwhelming. He tried to keep it simple—a trait we in The Wiggles admire more than most others—but at some point, it was inevitable that detail, jargon, and complexity would rear their ugly heads. So as he got to work pushing, prodding, manipulating, and unlocking muscles, bones, joints, and pressure points I never knew I had, I wanted to get to the "children's entertainer" version of his theory and approach.

Bring out the full-sized human specimen, please. No, there's no need for it to wear a Wiggles outfit. Thank you.

I'll ask the doc to step in and correct me if I get something wrong or dumb it down to such an extent I'm committing a crime, but here goes.

Think of the body as a spring. There are seven *floors* or platforms of this giant spring interconnected though the body, running toe to head.

Floor One: The arch of the foot or the master spring

Floor Two: Ankle joint #1—(subtalar joint)

Floor Three: Ankle joint #2—(ankle mortise)

Floor Four: The knee
Floor Five: The hip
Floor Six: The spine
Floor Seven: The spine-skull

This system is what protects and propels you as you take 10,000 steps a day, which equates to roughly 270 million collisions between foot and ground in a lifetime. If the muscles and other elements of the support for a floor are weak, damaged, or locked or if the spring is out of alignment, you're at acute risk of injury (and illness). Often pain is felt at the source of the problem, some of it due to inflammation (something that occurs chronically when the spring is damaged or ill-configured), although not all inflammation is immediately painful, which sometimes masks the origin and extent of the problem. Inflammation, initially a protective response of the body, eventually spreads through the system, inducing a range of reactions including a toxic effect that makes you more susceptible to a mind-boggling array of illnesses and afflictions.

Dr. Stoxen can tell by watching people walk if they have a locked or weak spring system and what problems it is causing. He's done the gait-watching analysis for leading physicians on-stage at major international conferences. The accuracy of his insight leaves them, like it did me, breathless and momentarily dumbstruck. You will find out how to analyze yourself in coming chapters.

By honing in on the source of the problem, the chances for a long-term *fix* are good. What's more, the flood of inflammatory toxins through the body can be stemmed.

His first focus in searching for answers is often the arches of your feet because a weakness or issue there has extreme implications for the entire mechanism. Consider, if you will, a multistory building. Problems, over time, may appear throughout the building—a crack in the wall on floor five; wear and tear on floor seven;

but if there's a major structural problem anywhere in the building, the first focus for an engineer is the foundation.

Yep, if you're built on a wonky foundation, or something destabilizing has happened down there, it's only a matter of time before you start to crumble—sorry, it is harsh but true. The great news is that if you know where to look for the problem, there's a very good chance you'll be able to correct it.

And now, quite possibly, you do.

It's not to say that the way most doctors currently assess and treat you is entirely wrong. But, because of how they are trained to view the human body, they often uncover only part of the truth about your condition. For example, over the years I seemed to have herniated discs more often than any other human being alive (OK, maybe not). Nevertheless, I would be diagnosed, provided with medication, and undergo some combination of rest and gentle therapy to alleviate me of the symptoms of that condition. The trouble was that the herniated disc was a locked spring on my "sixth level" and I had five more locked up down to my foundation, the master spring in my foot.

I didn't get the herniated disc because I picked up something heavy. I got it years before and it never healed because the root cause of my ailment (a locked spring in the foundation) was not even identified, let alone treated.

Put simply (really simply), doctors sometimes look only at the area on the body where you're having pain and rarely consider your body's structural issues—other than a conspicuous injury—when pondering the causes of the ailment. They're just not trained to look at the body the way Dr. Stoxen views it.

Modern medicine's approach is to carve up the body into different specializations. The specialists protect their turf—there's even laws ensuring others don't impinge on their territory. Unfortunately, that undermines the understanding that the body functions as an integrated system—a giant spring mechanism.

Anatomy of the Human Spring

I'll admit it, when the doc started talking about the human spring, I couldn't get this image out of my head of people coming down stairs like Slinkies.

Nevertheless, I could visualize the concept of the body quickly deteriorating if one part of the system is frozen or impeded. What I needed to know was, what actual parts make up "the spring?"

All of it, is the short answer—muscles and tendons, connective tissue, cartilage, joints, bones, muscles and tendons, and the arch of the foot.

These components are different *types* of springs, but they all interplay; they're all part of the grand plan.

The muscles and tendons, for example, are designed to stretch under load (before returning to their original shape) and are known as tension or extension springs, while the discs in the vertebrae are compression springs— they become shorter when force is applied.

The master spring—the arch of the foot—is a kind of leaf spring, from an engineering point of view. It resembles the same concept used in vehicle suspensions.

I am evidence of what can happen when the human spring locks or is impeded, but what is the big payoff for keeping this amazing mechanism healthy? Here's Dr. Stoxen's summary of the direct and immediate impact:

1. Soft landing, less shock to the skeleton
2. Ultimate efficiency and improved stamina, less energy required for movement
3. Increased speed and power of performance
4. Balance is improved
5. Improved agility in performance and coordination

6. Circulation improves, less spasm, allowing blood to flow more efficiently

7. Healthy alignment—healing potential is maximized

As we talk more about the process of restoring the spring, it'll become clear how these improvements have a profound impact on specific elements of health, fitness, and well-being—in ways you might not expect.

. . . .

Spreading the News

OK, so that's my layman's sketch of the situation. Next we'll take a look at what the doctor did to me, and for me, and hopefully more fully explain the mechanics of his approach before examining how that applies to you and your loved ones (and probably just about every family in your neighborhood).

But one more thing before I finish this little consultation with a song and dance. My ears are burning. I can hear you asking: "Why is the middle-aged children's entertainer telling me about this medical marvel and not my local doctor?"

I know you're asking that because for about five years I wondered why someone in the medical community wasn't flooding the media with this information. I got sick of waiting for that to happen, so I decided to write this book.

Truth is, Dr. Stoxen is spreading the word. As I mentioned earlier, experiencing his approach has been a valued perk of being a touring performer in the U.S. He's worked backstage with more than 300 entertainers, including some of the very biggest names in showbiz. But over the last decade the traditional medical community has been reaching out to him, too.

Recently he has traveled to countries such as Japan, Brazil, China, Mexico, and Great Britain, having accepted invitations to address about 50,000 medical doctors, specialists, and healers from scores of countries at some of the world's most prestigious medical conferences, including the Royal College of Physicians meeting in London, the SENS Conference in Cambridge, and the International Bangkok Congress on Anti-Aging. Chiropractors rarely receive such invitations.

The wheels of the establishment turn rather slowly, but the word is getting out. Sometimes it's hard to blow your own trumpet and maintain the focus on what's important—your work. On the other hand, if you've been helped—if your life has been changed like mine has—by that work, it's very difficult *not* to talk about it.

That's why I'm shouting it from the rooftops.

The Spring's the Thing

Before we launched into our marathon treatment sessions in Chicago, I was anxious to get a sense of how bad my situation was in the eyes of someone who understood my issues and had a plan to address them head on. Dr. Stoxen was appropriately diplomatic, using encouraging language and reminding me a positive approach was essential in the treatment and rehabilitation phases.

"Yeah, but Doc, I'm a big boy. Nothing will surprise me after years of being medicated and manipulated."

He gently recalled the analogy between the human spring mechanism and a multistory building and concluded: "You aren't yet at the stage of being condemned for structural instability, but your foundation is a mess and there's plenty of work to be done on other floors too."

Great, I thought, I'm a poorly constructed building.

Actually, the construction wasn't the big issue, it was the maintenance. I apparently was a classic case of someone who had been *regionally* examined and treated, meaning the focus of the rehabilitation I'd done over the years was generally in the vicinity of where I was experiencing pain, rather than where the pain was generated.

A chronic level of instability in the spine-back spring, as the doctor put it, would always be with me no matter how many adjustments, therapy sessions, and pills I received unless we got to the core problem, the lockup of my spring. I was waiting for the lengthy inspection of my back, but it never came. I know why now—if you've got neck pain, he's not necessarily going to work your neck; if you've got shin splints he's not going to treat your shins; instead he rebuilds you "from floor one to seven."

Pain, wherever it is located, is being generated by the fault in the spring system and the associated inflammation. Generally doctors will hone in on the area of the body where the discomfort is most concentrated—where most of the inflammation is centered. But this can be misleading, as the brain doesn't necessarily readily identify *silent* inflammation—pools of toxicity around the body, generated by the source of the injury. Dr. Stoxen says that silent inflammation is sometimes identifiable as those "knots" you didn't know were there until you have a rubdown. For the most part, it might be a dull pain you can't pinpoint.

Bottom line is that much inflammation—both obvious and silent—is generated by abnormal motion that is the result of a fault in the spring mechanism. Fix the fault and you stop the pain and, as a bonus, there is nothing standing in the way of the body healing itself of ailments. In turn that ensures efficient energy recycling as you move, reducing fatigue.

"I'm going to rebuild you from the ground up," he said as he plunged his fingers into the muscles in the arch of my foot.

"Ouch!" Clearly he'd gone straight to a problem spot.

Seeking a distraction from the treatment, I tried to get my head completely around this new theory about my perilous state. I mean, rebuild me, sure, but what specifically got me to this point of being a crumbling edifice? And I still don't fully get how structural issues make me sick. What terrible thing, besides getting a bit plump, did I do to weaken the muscles around my arches, anyway? He'd explained earlier that my pronator-super-thingos had failed me and that my arches had collapsed inward, but what sin was I committing when I walked to make this happen?

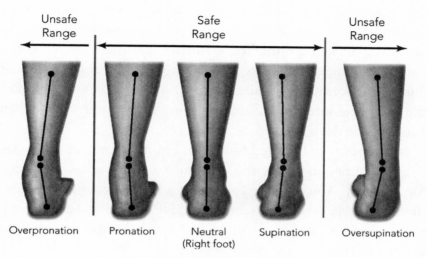

Unsafe Range	Safe Range	Unsafe Range

Overpronation   Pronation   Neutral (Right foot)   Supination   Oversupination

Safe and unsafe foot roll on landing.

"I've got two words for you," he said. "Pronation and supination."

Well, that explains it . . . Fortunately, he elaborated.

"The way your foot rolls when it impacts the ground stressed and strained the support muscles over time."

He explained that body weight is absorbed by the spring, but the efficiency of that process is dependent, in part, on how the foot rolls when it touches the ground. The roll should distribute weight across the foot so it is absorbed gradually, avoiding shock to the skeleton. It rolls from supination (the outside of the foot) to pronation (the inside).

That roll has to be performed within a safe range, meaning if it starts rolling too far on the outside or too far to the inside, it causes the lower leg limb to twist, imposing abnormal stress and strain through the muscles, ligaments, and tendons of the knee, hip, ankle, lower back, lower spine, and up through the head.

The spring suspension muscles in the arch of the foot must be strong in order to prevent overrolling (oversupination or overpronation) and to maintain the foot in a safe range.

"Your spring suspension system muscles that support your arches fatigued and weakened. The arch spring eventually collapsed and locked and that led to further abnormalities in the way you move, imposing stress and strain on all muscles, ligament joints, and bones. Eventually, the wear and tear on every joint in the body promotes the inflammation—which is nothing less than a tool of the devil."

Oh, come on, I scoffed to myself, but my face gave me away.

"Inflammation causes the constant pain, the aches, and brain fog," he said. "You feel like you've got a bit of a cold all the time, right?" *How did he know?* "Chemically, inflammation—it's like poison . . . it *is* poison. It is a toxin that flows through your system causing cells to become distressed. It causes pain and exhaustion, and even contributes to feelings of hopelessness and depression. Inflammation is one of the greatest accelerants in the aging process and leads to many diseases associated with 'getting old.' In fact, he went on to say, many doctors feel that chronic inflammation is a more logical contributing factor to heart disease than high cholesterol.

I was not happy about the news, but for the first time in decades, I could follow the pattern of causality. I still wasn't expecting miracles, but any sort of relief would be welcome. Hey, I was just surprised and pleased to be included in the explanation of my own diagnosis.

"It's a three-step process: We unlock you, we strengthen the spring, and eventually supercharge it," he said. "That's a sizable journey but we start by identifying all the weaknesses in your mechanism."

Dr. Stoxen had also honed in on a flaw in the spring suspension support in my pelvis. The lower back is stacked on the pelvis and the pelvis is suspended by muscles that move it in six different directions: front, back, left side motion, right side motion, and right and left twisting. Despite the fact I have always been physically active, my muscles were weak. Eventually I'd need a specific routine to strengthen them to adequately suspend the pelvis in the right position, taking away the stress and strain that caused the inflammation and pain.

How time flies when you're being manipulated!

When I was called to the stage I didn't exactly leap off the treatment table, but incredibly I was able to get up without assistance and walk, even dance, without pain. It was only the beginning, but I already felt relatively transformed. Readying myself for the show, the doctor made an unusual request.

"Take a close look at your audience today—the little ones up the front—I want to point something out to you later."

Sure, you're the doc.

With that, I literally skipped onto the stage.

Biomechanic Crash and Burn

Got chronic arthritis? Joint pain anywhere? Check your feet!

It's not the first thing that comes to mind and certainly traditional approaches to healing don't make that connection, but Dr. Stoxen's model demands an inspection of the master spring should the body be operating dysfunctionally. Rather than thinking in terms of medical terminology and traditional analysis, it helps to envision your musculoskeletal self as a mechanical engineer or physicist might.

I'll let Dr. Stoxen explain:

As a spring, you are built to change in shape when your body impacts the ground. The energy generated is stored in the spring then released as you regain your original shape. That's what should happen naturally when you move.

The perfect spring load and unload is known as elastic (or temporary) deformity. The deformity, in this instance, refers to the change in shape, for example, when you push down on an old bedspring. Similarly, when you take a step, the human spring deforms in shape, storing the energy. As your foot comes off the ground the spring unloads elastically (releasing the energy) and shifts back to the *exact* original shape. That's the process with every healthy step, jump, bound, skip, running impact, triple flip, even one of Anthony's "Wiggly" dances.

If this natural process of elastic deformity is altered or restricted it has repercussions for the entire mechanism. Over time—remember every step deforms the spring which, over a year, is approximately 3.6 million impacts— even if the abnormal motion is subtle, it can lead to a plastic (or permanent) deformity.

This means the force of the foot landing is loading into the human spring when it is weak, stiff, locked, or in a motion that is contrary to the way it was designed to move.

Back to the trusty bedspring: What happens when you continuously squeeze it down from the wrong angle? Over time, you bend it. The same thing happens to the human springs or joints in the body; they don't return to their original shape. It's permanent damage. The permanent deformities manifest themselves as bunions, torn or worn cartilage, or herniated discs.

The other negative is that a damaged human spring doesn't have the same capacity to load and release as much energy as it did before the plastic deformity, which means you end up with a loss in performance and natural energy, otherwise known as *aging*.

And that's what leads to the "use to be able to-s": I used to be able to run, walk for miles, bend over, get out of a chair, run a marathon, or dance like Fred Astaire.

It is part of the reason athletes lose a step in pace and performance when they hit their 30s, often forcing retirement. In our 40s and 50s this process can happen much faster, often leading to permanent disability.

To get a sense about how impactful a lack of spring can be, think how difficult it is to run in sand. The spring energy is deadened on the soft surface so when you run you lose that free energy. This forces a switch to other muscles to propel you, using more energy and making you tire faster.

Of course, a spring can lock in a compromised position anywhere in the mechanism, not just in the arches of the feet—either way, because all "floors" of the body make up an interconnected spring mechanism, it has a domino effect of imposing stress and strain throughout the body, inducing a potential riot of seemingly unrelated conditions.

Anthony had already endured nearly all of these symptoms and ailments when I first met him.

Take a look and see if any apply to you. If so, welcome to the club. It's not terribly exclusive, there are hundreds of millions of members around the world, and that number is growing daily as sedentary modern lifestyles and habits accelerate our disintegration.

Arch pain

Plantar fasciitis

Heel spurs

Ankle swelling/pain

Shin splints

Calf cramps

Chronic knee pain

Knee joint degeneration

Iliotibial band syndrome

Poor circulation (spasmed muscles choke off circulation)

Varicose veins

Hip pain

Hip joint degeneration

Lower back pain

Herniated discs (that don't heal)

Upper back pain

Chronic headaches

Furthermore, if your entire human spring is sprung from floors one to seven for a long time, as many are, the bang and twist with every step that imposes stress and strain causes inflammation on every floor leading to symptoms often misdiagnosed as fibromyalgia. Also, the loss of the free spring energy, the drag on the joints, and the toxic levels of inflammation could lead to a misdiagnosis of chronic fatigue syndrome, while the nervous system, firing 24/7 to signal to the muscles to contract and lock the spring (spasms) can be misdiagnosed as restless leg syndrome.

At night your nervous system should shut down to allow you some restful sleep, but that is impossible when your spring is locked. It's little wonder that people coping with a locked mechanism often suffer from insomnia.

Also, when your gait is impacted, your calf muscle does not contract properly—an important obstacle in pumping blood back to the heart. By restoring the human spring and relearning healthy walking patterns circulation improves.

If you believe you have one of these conditions and it won't leave you, consider the possibility of a misdiagnosis and the very real possibility you have a locked spring. It won't immediately ease your pain but maybe it's a long sought after, plausible explanation for your extreme fatigue. After all, if your spring mechanism is locked it's like dragging yourself through sand as you take the average of 10,000 steps each day, and over time, that's going to leave a mark—doing the sort of damage all doctors struggle to reverse.

Just Like a Kid

Back on the table for a long session after the first Chicago shows, the doctor resumed the spring release process. Having already noticed a distinct positive change I wondered aloud about how long the ultimate repair and rejuvenation of my spring would take.

Being a chronic patient, I always suspect I'll be made aware of the long recovery time, so the answer surprised me. While recharging and "supercharging" the spring would be an ongoing project, the doctor insisted only a few more marathon sessions would be required to restore my spring to its natural healthy state. That's right, 25 years of chronic pain gone; natural energy recovered, blood flowing freely, strength boosted and, most important, "hope" and a bit of lost faith in the medical profession fully restored.

"The spring will be restored in a couple of weeks and there won't be anything getting in the way of the healing process," he said. "That's a fault with many traditional approaches; they don't work to repair the body's mechanics to the way they were engineered to function—eliminating the thing getting in the way of natural spring.

"Instead, the problem is merely masked with medication, or the area with the highest level of inflammation is treated at the expense of the core issue. Once you develop a tolerance for medication, you notice the pain is still there, so the only thing to do, they think, is to give you even more medication." Ah, the familiar cycle of pain-medication-pain-more medication-more pain-even more medication. I know it well.

Over the years, I also became an experienced hand at the futile routine of experiencing terrible back pain—getting an MRI, receiving back treatment (injections, adjustments, and massages), and exercising muscles to support the back. Then one day, usually just as I'm starting to feel OK, I am doubled over with back pain again for no apparent reason.

I really couldn't take any more of that. Not only is it frustrating and exhaustingly painful, you start to doubt yourself. You wonder perhaps if it's something weird you're doing to induce the pain. And after a while, if you're seeing the same doctor, he or she starts to hint at that, too. I was thrilled just to have a constructive plan of attack. In my sessions with Dr. Stoxen he would treat all seven floors of my spring, starting with the 33 joints that surround the 26 bones in the arch of the feet and ankles. He did this by manipulating specific points (his secret spots which I'll reveal later), sometimes working on a particular area for hours at a time.

Once all the joints are released, the spring regains its normal "bounce" as the force of each impact between foot and ground is spread across all joints, ensuring a smoother ride. Wear and tear on joints, muscles, tendons, and ligaments abate. And around-the-clock muscle spasms that contribute to fatigue subside—no more eight-coffee days or sugar-laden pick-me-up drinks.

I'd have to learn to "walk" again and make sure I exercised appropriately to strengthen my spring and the supporting muscles, but I was up for the challenge.

"I'll be like a spring chicken," I joked.

"Or a preschooler at a Wiggles concert," the doctor suggested. "Did you watch the kids closely today?" I had, at his request, although our show is always interactive. We talk with the children throughout, and regularly hop off the stage to say hi. The little ones dance frantically alongside their family and friends.

"They can really move," he observed. "Great spring in their step, wouldn't you say?"

Indeed.

Kids' spring mechanisms are usually pristine and their natural inclination to run, bounce, skip, hop, and jump reflects that. "Ever noticed how children take a hard fall then, a few minutes later, after tears and a kiss from mom, they're back at it, running around as if nothing happened?" the doctor asked. "They have protection—a fully functioning human spring.

"If it's us, the old folks, we're waking up stiff in the morning, maybe needing a bit of physical therapy, even a painkiller. And, of course, it becomes chronic pain, maybe leaving us with a permanent limp or inability to romp about like we were only weeks before, and a long-term pill-popping habit."

The advantage of youth in this respect is not only that they have yet to wear down their spring mechanism, they effectively train it every day, as they run barefoot in every direction—small sessions of plyometric perfection.

"I can't say I've met many kids with fibromyalgia or a herniated disc that won't heal," he said.

In many ways the aim of the Human Spring Approach is to facilitate the restoration of that natural youthful vigor and boundless energy, giving us our spring back, quite literally, and eliminating inflammation that contributes to limiting us physically and mentally by accelerating the aging process and fueling diseases of aging, including:

- Skin degeneration
- Heartburn
- Feeling older than you are/depression
- Some cancers
- Fatigue
- Food addictions and eating disorders, weight gain, obesity, and food cravings
- Circulatory diseases such as atherosclerosis (hardening of the arteries), heart attack, and stroke
- Inflammatory bowel diseases
- Neurological diseases, such as Parkinson's disease and Alzheimer's disease
- Periodontal disease
- Respiratory diseases: asthma, chronic bronchitis
- Rheumatic diseases: fibromyalgia, osteoarthritis, systemic lupus, scleroderma

There are also indirect links with numerous metabolic diseases, hormonal imbalances, and depression.

I have to admit, it was all a bit spooky. I mean, Dr. Stoxen was saying that if he fixed my spring my pain would go away, I wouldn't be tired all the time, I wouldn't get headaches, I'd finally get rid of the fibromyalgia symptoms, stifle the aging process, thwart serious diseases associated with aging, and maybe even get the upper hand after years of suffering depression.

Yeah, right.

"How's that feel?" he asked, after he'd finished his squeezing—stretching—pulling—twisting of my foundation.

"Well, I've still got to deal with the back pain, you barely touched me there . . ." I started. "Hey! . . . I don't feel anything—it's gone!" I was overwhelmed, to say the least, by the level of immediate improvement.

Three more long, long stints on the treatment table would follow, but after several days of work, I was bouncing onto the stage and swinging my old hips like Elvis (prior to the peanut-butter-and-banana-binge stage).

Oh, and the thought about opting out of The Wiggles? Just a memory. A bad memory, like my hazy recollection of what it was like to experience daily pain.

5

Putting Humpty
Together Again

When you're hurting, or ill, it's not just a painful and
inconvenient state to be in, it's positively lonely.
You don't want to be a burden on other people, so
you suffer in silence without end, trying any and every "remedy"
you can get your hands on—it's often a prescribed drug that ends
up being ineffective and, as in my case, makes you more isolated
and desperate.

My encounter with Dr. Stoxen had liberated me from that
mind-set in a number of ways. I immediately threw out every
pain-killer I had. And, believe me, that was a big step, as I'd been
using the stupid things for years.

I also came to understand I wasn't in this alone. As I celebrated
the prospect of shutting down the pain that had plagued me for
years, I got to appreciate that I was surrounded by people who in
many ways were going through exactly what I had gone through.

Comfortable with the fact I was on the road to recovery, I opened up to friends and family, members of The Wiggles cast, our dedicated crew, and some of our fans about the personal health battles I'd been having. Much to my astonishment, many people revealed they'd been facing similar issues over the years. They related their own issues: neck pain, chronic headaches, bad backs, shin splints, even failed surgeries—situations that had forced them to retire prematurely or to make other extreme and radical lifestyle changes.

In fact, millions of people have at least some of the same challenges as I and unfortunately that number is swelling daily. We are in the midst of a number of epidemics, none more dangerous than obesity.

About 65 percent of people in North America (one in three children!) and a similar number in Australia and Great Britain are overweight or obese. The extra weight is putting pressure on the muscles that suspend the arches of the feet and other floors of the human spring. Chronic pain is already a burden for 70 million people in the U.S.—soon it will impact millions more.

Even if you've managed to keep the weight down, afflictions such as fibromyalgia, diabetes, and chronic fatigue are handcuffing many of us as we try to live life well. But come in close and listen: There's a way to turn things around. *You can fix this.*

A Plan of Action

Right, I know what you're going to say—you try to exercise and eat right. You've read the books by the latest gurus, you're following those "complete guides," religiously doing the old upper and lower body strengthening exercises, working your core with crunches, and following instructions to improve leg strength and flexibility.

Alternatively, some of you are, well, kind of stuck in front of the television. You know, the kids are screaming, work is barking at you to come in early tomorrow . . . so inaction seems the best course of action; there is no time for exercise right now, but you'll get there soon.

Hey, I don't doubt that. At least 20 million of you will start a jogging program this year. Congratulations. Running is one of the best ways to get and stay fit and is a vital anti-aging tool. Trouble is, because many people start their fitness campaigns assuming they still have the same "spring" in their step they had decades ago, millions will sustain an injury before the first twelve months of the fitness program are up. And, man, is that frustrating! You're trying to do the right thing . . . maybe you're just getting too old, maybe you should give it up . . . or maybe you should look at your feet!

Sorry I shouted; just wanted to make the point. Again.

Actually, it's not just your landing gear we need to look at, it's your walk. There's no use planning a fitness regime to rival an Olympic athlete unless you first sort out how healthy or otherwise your gait is. You may be able to fly on the track but it's not going to take too long before you're grounded permanently if every step you take is the equivalent of a crash landing. In fact, even if you strive to run with proper form and technique you still could be doing yourself more harm than good (like many of those millions who started and stopped a jogging campaign in the last year). The key is the integrity of the human spring. If you're exercising on a weak or locked spring, you're setting yourself up to do damage down the track, if not immediately.

So let's walk before we run.

Rightly, parents everywhere celebrate long and hard when their kids take their first steps. I know we did. Learning to walk is an epic milestone, though it's just as important to learn how to walk properly again after we've put a few miles in.

Let's do a bit of road testing to see how healthy your spring is and give you a feel for what you might be doing right or wrong with every step. If I had the same level of understanding about the human spring as Dr. Stoxen, I would be analyzing gaits in detail at every opportunity—I'd make it a party trick; it's that startling. Unfortunately, I can't tell from watching someone walk *exactly* what is wrong with them, but using the list of common flaws Dr. Stoxen has compiled, it is relatively easy to conclude whether someone's spring is being compromised. You'll be surprised at how accurately you can assess whether someone is suffering from chronic pain and which side it's on.

Make use of this with your family by watching how those flip-flop wearing kids of yours walk or observing your husband who's been recently complaining of back pain on the left side. Watch closely when your always-tired mother-in-law, with the sore hips, shuffles in to visit next time. I'll guarantee their doctors aren't doing this. (Maybe you should diplomatically suggest they read the book and try it before prescribing your loved ones another pill for pain?)

So, come on, over to the mirror. Nobody's looking, take off those shoes. Leave the socks on if you must.

Now, walk.

Oh, dear me! See how your feet point outward? You're waddling like a duck. Think about it! Your feet are pointing one way while your body moves in another direction. Maybe you've noticed your beloved husband has been duck walking too since he put on those extra fifteen pounds, right? No worries. I was the same. I was waddling around for ages. I had to learn how to *walk* again.

The key is to keep the feet straight. Point the second toe on each foot toward the target/destination and keep them aimed in that direction as you step. This allows the spring to land squarely on the ground, maintaining the alignment of your joints, preventing unnecessary wear and tear.

When you walk with your feet out, it creates enormous stress on major skeletal connections from toe to head: ankles, knees, hips, lower back, and neck. Eventually, this is going to wear away at cartilage, and, for example, if you put on more weight, the deterioration of the joints accelerates, often leading to the medical necessity of joint replacement, according to Dr. Stoxen.

Right, stay there. A quick exercise: Wiggle your toes; now use your feet to "write" the alphabet. If you can't get to Z without your feet getting tired, then the muscles in your feet need work. So maybe the duck walk isn't an issue and your feet aren't tired after the A to Z test but you're not out of the woods yet.

Here are some more potentially harmful habits to look for:

Toe Up: Lifting Toes Prior to Landing

You should not be able to see the underside of your feet when you walk. If you can it may be because you're pointing your toes up just before landing and they're probably staying raised on contact with the ground.

Chances are you wear sandals or flip-flops a lot. Remember when you first wore them? They kept falling off, so in all likelihood you started raising the toes to keep them on. This compromises the spring loading process because you're tightening the suspension system before impact. Every step is a "bang"producing pains and problems such as shin splints and plantar fasciitis.

Model Walk: Walking with Feet Too Close Together

Yes, daaaaaarling, you probably deserve to be on a catwalk somewhere, but don't do the model walk. Walking with the feet closer together than what's considered mechanically sound could stress the ankle joints, knees, hips, and lower back. It may trigger spasms that weaken, stiffen, and potentially lock the spring mechanism.

If you can't tell you're a candidate by walking toward the mirror (please resist the urge to sashay) check your shoes in the closet. If your feet are getting too close to each other, they actually collide on occasions, often leaving scuff marks on footwear.

Pirate Peg Walk: Walking with Stiff Feet and Ankles

Me hearties, I tested this on me Wiggles pirate character, Captain Feathersword, and I'm pleased to say, he failed miserably. Lucky for him, arghh.

The pirate peg walk is when your ankle and foot are locked up stiff. You swing your leg through and your foot and ankle don't release or move. They're just a solid unit that bangs on the ground, the body weight rolling over the top of a stiff "peg-leg." As the foot comes off the ground it doesn't even bend and there's no obvious spring. It's just bang and lift, bang and lift. Arghh, I mean, ouch!

Horse Clop Walk: Pounding through the Walk

I don't know if this is scientifically proven to happen when you're trying to relax with a coffee (strong espresso, please), but I suspect someone will eventually do a study.

It's a quiet, private café, you're about to take the first sip, and THUD, THUD, THUD. The sound of a horse clopper— maybe it's a big guy or maybe it's a 100-pound woman in high-heeled shoes—but they're the same. They are banging their foot down with each step as if they're on a campaign to kill an intrusion of scurrying cockroaches (and you can guess how I feel about that).

It's probably no surprise that banging sends shockwaves through the musculoskeletal system, causing shin splints, among other things. Pound down hard enough, you're going to shake something loose, that's for sure. Focus on *landing* your foot rather than banging it down and concentrate on letting it spring lightly off the ground—especially if you plan to come back to my favorite café.

Short Step Walk: Walking with a Short Stride

Question: Have you ever walked behind the six-foot-tall guy who takes steps like he's a 4-foot-11-inch girl?
Answer: Not for long.

That's because he's taking forever to get anywhere and he's doing his spring mechanism no favors in doing so. His foot should be springing off the ground, propelling him toward a stride length that's proportional to his height, but because it's likely locked, he has to *lift* the foot.

Also, with no follow through, his calves are not contracting as much as they should; meaning blood is not being pumped to his heart as it might. Potentially, circulation issues will arise.

Short-strider should focus on not lifting his foot prematurely. Gently tell him to follow through and let the spring work its magic.

Twist Toes: Rather Than Springing, the Foot Twists

After landing, the foot should "bounce" back up, but if your spring mechanism isn't working properly, your foot compensates by twisting under your body weight to get energy from elsewhere in order to get it off the ground again. Not only is this tiring and inefficient, it strains the ankle, knee joint, knee cap, the outside hip, and the lower back.

Weak Ankle Walk: The Ankle Isn't Sitting Directly Over the Foot

With each step, the ankle and foot look like they want to head in different directions. The second toe, ankle, and shin bone should be aligned. Instead, the ankle has a bow in it rather than sitting upright over the foot.

A counter support shoe is usually required to start the strengthening process, in conjunction with spring suspension system exercises and carefully constructed running drills.

There is no one way to walk. Our gaits can be very different and still be healthy, but these traits are signs you have a locked spring mechanism. The more you walk with an abnormal gait, the more the spring locks (from protective spasms). Simply try and adjust your landing and stride to avoid these obvious flaws, using the second toe as your compass. Keep your shins loose when walking, and be conscious of trying to land your foot in a stress-free manner. This relaxes the arch and other floors of the spring, allowing the force of impact to load efficiently, protecting you from crash landings and improving efficiency of movement, preserving your joints, and boosting energy.

Locked Spring Self-Examination

OK, fellow duck-walkers and others, we'll come back to a few more ways to improve your gait later. But from the look of things, you really need to verify whether your spring is locked. Ideally you'd have a professional inspect your spring, but since Dr. Stoxen is booked up until 2020 or something, that might be tough, so let's take a look together now. I regularly do these self-examinations, taught to me by the doctor, even though I'm confident I've overcome many of the issues I used to have.

You'll probably have a pretty good idea if you're locked up without having to inspect your feet or doing a gait inspection. Chronic pain anywhere is a leading indicator and certainly just a lack of "springiness" in your step is usually useful evidence. Even if your sole complaint is fatigue, there's a good chance it's due to a locked spring.

Now, take a look for bunions or other physical anomalies on your feet. If there are any of these "plastic deformities" glaring back at you, we have issues.

Regardless, let's try any one or more of these tests.

The Arch Wiggle Test

No, it's not named after the mysterious fifth Wiggle.

You're going to wiggle each toe to see how much movement it produces. Hold and stabilize the long toe bones at the midfoot.

Start with the little toe—the movement is usually quite pronounced. If any of the toes are tight and difficult to manipulate, or if they seem to wiggle smoothly only to abruptly stop (and crack or click) it's a sign of stiffening, weak, or locked arch springs. In particular, the second and third digits—the toes next to the big toe—are the most likely to be frozen.

Calcium Check

Use your fingers to find calcium deposits in your foot. Feel the big toe; you're looking for a protrusion where the long toe bone joins with the midfoot bones. If you discover a hard bump, it's probably a calcium buildup caused by constant inflammation generated as the foot locks/unlocks. The calcium deposit will stay with you—it is of no concern, but it indicates you have had a locked spring at some time in life—maybe now.

The Foot-Ankle Alignment Test (front view)

Back to the mirror, please. Stand up straight and do a little jig. OK, that has nothing to do with this test, but it's always healthy to have a bit of dance.

Right, back to it. Draw an imaginary line from your second toe running up through your ankle to your knee. Is the line straight or is it broken around the ankle area? If it's broken, then the muscles that suspend your arch spring or your foot are probably not strong enough and your spring system could be damaged.

The Foot-Ankle Alignment Test (back view)

Turn around so your back is facing the mirror. If you can look over your shoulder and see the back of your feet we'll proceed, otherwise get a friend in here with a camera and get them to take a snapshot of the back view of your legs. Yes, yes, I know, it must be a trusted friend.

Draw an imaginary line from the feet, through the heel bone, and up to the back of the knees. Again, check to see if it's straight.

The Foot-Ankle on Tip-Toe Test.

Facing front again, get up on your toes. If your ankle is over the top of your toes in a straight line, then both your supination and pronation muscles are strong. If the foot twists to the side, then you have an imbalance in the strain between the supinators and the pronators, creating weakness. That means instead of a "square" movement you may be twisting your foot when it pushes off the ground, potentially causing stress on the muscles and ligaments and wear on the joints. (You may be twisting around an already locked spring.)

Another quick test is to *listen*. No, not to your doctor, you've been doing that for years, but to your feet. Stick your fingers in your ears, take a stroll, and listen to every step. The louder the *thump* or *thud* emanating from your feet, the harder the landing, which may be because your spring is locked.

Finally, time to check your balance. It doubles as a sobriety test. Face the mirror; stand on one foot, lifting the other leg up to a 90 degree angle. Try to keep the middle of your hips, chest, and head steady and centered. If you're unable to hold the pose it could be a sign of weak or spasmed muscles (or excessive wine consumption).

When I did this in front of Dr. Stoxen on our first meeting, I lurched about like a drunken lunatic. Then, after just one marathon treatment session, I did it again—I barely moved an inch.

All of the above tests will give you a good indication whether your arch spring is locked, weak, or stiff. Even if you only have one "issue" it's quite possible that over time it will start to limit your exercise and daily leisure activities and cause damage to your joints.

If you noticed you had a few signs of locked arches, the time for action is right now in order to avoid the kind of damage that could result in a level of disability, even joint replacement surgery.

What Can You Do?

You can start helping yourself by unlocking the master spring. Take a take a close look at the photographs and use them as a guide and follow Dr. Stoxen's instructions below.

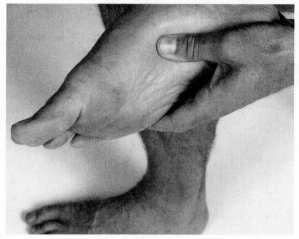

Release Toe Spring #1.

Release Toe Spring #1: Apply pressure to the base of the big toe in the midarch. Move up the length of the big toe one thumb print at a time.

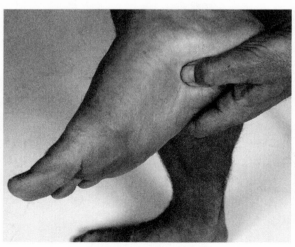

Release Toe Spring #2.

Release Toe Spring #2: Apply pressure between the big toe and the second toe at the midarch. Move up the length of the toe.

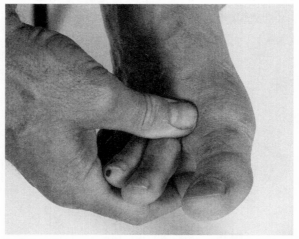

Release Plantar Calcaneoavicular (The Spring Ligament).

Release Plantar Calcaneoavicular (The Spring Ligament): Apply pressure at the base of the area between the second toe and the third toe in the midarch. Move up the length of the third toe.

Release Male Bunion: Apply pressure on the inside arc of the big toe at the joint. Work all tender areas around the joint.

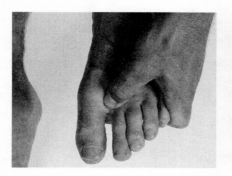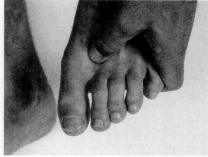

Release Toe Spring #1 and #2.

Release Toe Spring #1 and #2: Apply pressure at the base of the space between the big and second toes. Move the length of the web area between toes.

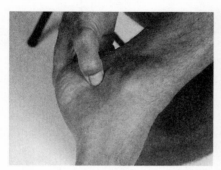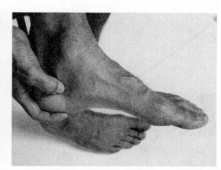

Release Ankle Joint #1 Spring (Subtalar).

Release Ankle Joint #1 Spring (Subtalar): Apply pressure at the ankle joint. Wiggle foot and ankle to feel the joint line. Move up the length of the joint.

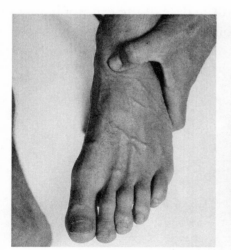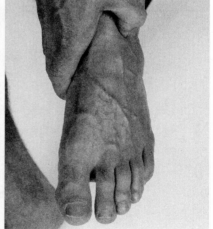

Release Ankle Joint #2 Spring (Ankle Mortise).

Release Ankle Joint #2 Spring (Ankle Mortise): Find the crevasse of the ankle joint. Apply pressure, then move along the joint line.

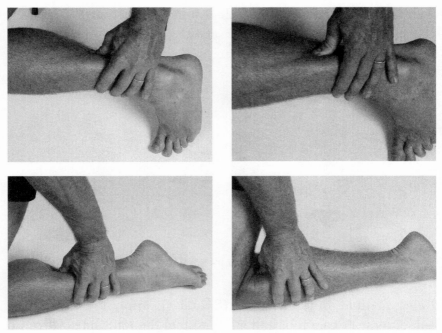

Release Calf and Arch Spring.

Release Calf and Arch Spring: At the base of the calf, apply pressure to the joint. Move up the joint line to the back of the knee.

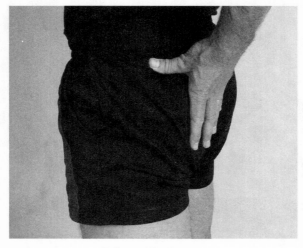

Release Hip Spring.

Release Hip Spring: Find the crest of the hip just below the waistline. Apply pressure, and then follow a path along the crest to the tailbone. Move down to the bottom of the tailbone.

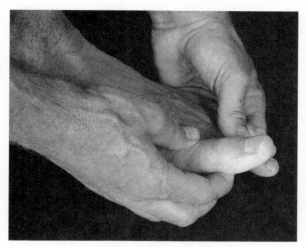

Stretch Scissor Toe.

Stretch Scissor Toe: Grasp the big and second toes and scissor them up and down to stretch the fascia between them. Repeat with each toe.

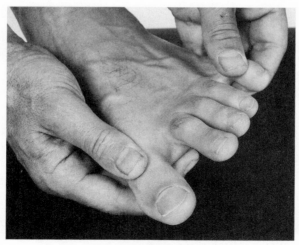

Stretch Toe Separation.

Stretch Toe Separation: Hold the big toe and each of the other toes starting with the little toe. Pull them apart for about three seconds at a time.

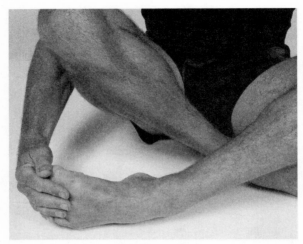

Stretch Plantar Flexion.

Stretch Plantar Flexion: Align fingers with toes. Pull the toes into plantar flexion to increase the depth of the arch.

Stretch Dorsiflexion.

Stretch Dorsiflexion: Wrap a towel around the top half of the foot and pull the foot into dorsiflexion.

For all of these exercises, use your thumb to apply slight pressure down to the bone, if possible, in the designated areas; you'll know when you've hit the exact spot—if you have inflamed ligaments or muscles in that area there will be some pain. Don't worry, you are not causing damage. It hurts because the muscles are stiff and inflamed. Now, gently apply pressure with your thumb or finger and hold it. The pain can be quite sharp, especially if you have had the condition for a while. But don't panic; after about two to three minutes, the discomfort starts to subside. The pain will come and go in waves a few times and eventually all you feel is pressure. If you don't hold the point until all the pain goes away, you will feel sore in these areas the next day. Don't shortchange the technique. Move on to the next spot.

Measure the area you are treating using your thumb print—it's called a Chinese inch. Move one Chinese inch at a time until you have covered the entire area. You may feel a rush of blood and energy through the treated area.

Once you have hit all the secret spots, your arch spring may be loose enough to be "unlocked."

- Stand on tip-toes (making sure your ankle and shin bones line up straight above the balls of the feet and are not twisted to the side). Do this ten to fifteen times and you will likely both feel and hear the foot and ankle muscles pull the bones back to where they are supposed to be. With each crack or click, the feet and ankles get looser— when you don't hear that sound for about five repetitions, stop. The muscles have done all the resetting they can for now.

- Stretch the arch down by grabbing each side of the mid-arches with your hands; then wiggle them loose. If you really get it, you'll feel and hear a click with the release of a toe joint, usually in the first and second toes, as these are the most common areas where the arches lock.

Do the routines above at least once a day, and always right before exercise of any kind. If you've been on your feet all day, do this routinely at night before you go to bed. Your feet will feel springy in the morning.

Keep in mind, the process is akin to taking a piece of frozen steak and thawing it with your bare hands, so it's a physical challenge. For example, it took several days of hard work to unlock Anthony's spring, so don't expect complete or immediate success when you do this yourself. Nevertheless, please, persevere. You can perform these procedures anywhere and at any time, but occasionally make time to treat yourself to a long session (hours long).

If you suspect or know your spring is locked, it's vitally important to rectify the situation completely before launching into a training program, otherwise you may be doing yourself more harm than good. In fact, you can *accelerate* the aging process if you exercise on a locked spring mechanism. Even walking or gentle jogging can be harmful—it's no coincidence that many people break down soon after they start a running regime.

Those Extra Pounds

Dr. Stoxen is probably too diplomatic to say it, but take it from Zumo, if you're investing the time and making the effort to unlock your spring, give some serious thought to your diet, too. It took me months to work though my issues, but when I realized I had a chance to break the cycle of illness and injury courtesy of a fully functioning spring for the first time in years, I sensed an urgent need not to waste the opportunity to initiate a complete turnaround.

Dropping a few pounds through sensible eating can be the icing on the cake as you steel yourself to make up for all that lost time dealing with chronic pain. Without excess weight, your spring has the potential to function as it was designed and that's a big step toward the ultimate goal of getting into a position to realize your potential or at least to be as ambitious as you want to be. You may not want to be an elite athlete; you might like being a couch potato, but at least give yourself a choice.

Shoe Time

By the end of our Chicago sojourn, I was already feeling like a new man. I could walk, run, dance, jump—even smile again. (I wish I could have celebrated with a big dinner but I was still battling horrendous stomach and digestive ailments.)

I had a few more marathon sessions over the following weeks with Dr. Stoxen before putting into place a stretch and exercise routine designed to strengthen the spring. After that, he planned a program to "supercharge" it. We'll detail those easy-to-follow routines in these pages. During the course of the long treatment sessions, I came to understand that a central component of Dr. Stoxen's approach was to identify habits and behaviors that contribute to the human spring being compromised, from the way we move and what exercises we're doing, to how much weight we're carrying, even what we we're wearing.

When he inspected the cushioned, high-tech dancing shoes I used to wear on stage every day he looked at them with the kind of disgust one reserves for a rare viewing of something unspeakable. I also saw him examining the footwear other cast members were wearing—he didn't look happy.

Dr. Stoxen is unapologetically "anti-shoe"—any shoe—for reasons we'll soon explore in detail. But he is practical enough to understand that most of us would probably induce curious looks if we showed up in the workplace, or for that vital meeting, sans footwear. So unless you can convince the whole office to throw their shoes out (and believe me, I've tried), the next best step is to at least ensure your footwear is fitted professionally and provides appropriate support so the foot doesn't overroll (collapse into overpronation or oversupination). A stabilized heel is vital in this regard, whether you stand on flat hard surfaces most of the day or fling yourself around a stage like I do.

Like many of the experienced dancers in our cast I used to purchase shoes based on how they looked and the desire to be "as comfortable as possible," which athletic-shoe manufacturers, in particular, tell you translates into a shoe that will "absorb the shock of impact." I applied those criteria when selecting street wear shoes, too—until I met Anti-Shoe Doctor Stoxen, that is.

Claims of "comfort" and "support" with most shoes, it seems, are about as accurate as saying deep-fried food has health advantages. Admittedly it's relative; if you haven't eaten for a month, fried food might be an option and Dr. Stoxen would probably suggest that if you have to walk on glass, a shoe might prove useful.

"Shoes terrorize the feet," he said.

The shoe and foot engage in a battle—the foot wanting to go one way and the footwear insisting on taking it in another direction, leading to deformities in the spring from which it cannot "bounce" back. The (natural) basic engineering has been changed. Also, when you wear footwear, nature's normal support mechanisms in the foot do not have to work, leading to atrophy (wasting away), and causing weakness in the spring suspension system.

Furthermore, the foot was designed to accept the weight of the body across the 33 joints and 26 bones—with many flexible joints it can distribute forces over a wider time frame (as it rolls), lessening the jarring impact. Shoes, however, process the generated force differently. With footwear—even high-tech running shoes, according to recent surveys—the impact of the landing is distributed with greater force, even though some shoe manufacturers would have you think the opposite.

By wearing shoes you transform the foot into a solid unit rather than allowing it to be the flexible foundation it was designed to be to reduce stress during landing and takeoff. Hard landings cause shock to the skeleton, and while it might seem like heavily cushioned shoes would be the answer, they are, in fact, likely doing more damage, as they dramatically affect the arch spring's ability to appropriately absorb, store, then release the energy from each step. Rather than strapping five-inch pillows to your feet, the best solution is to repair the spring mechanism in the arches by following the procedures and exercises in this book.

Meanwhile, if you must wear shoes—and my latest spot survey indicates most people feel they must from time to time— have them fitted by someone who knows what they are doing, whether you're a performer, waiter, bus driver, or mother. This is no simple task. Even if the shoe salesperson knows his or her business, mass production of footwear in recent years means choice of shoe sizes is often limited. Increasingly, half sizes 8.5 or 9.5 are hard to come by. Instead, you're squeezed into an 8 or a 9, or in some cases, stores only keep even numbers, so an 8 or a 10 will have to do. Surveys have found up to 80 percent of women don't wear the right shoe size on occasion.

Under the doctor's watchful eye, I procured two new pairs of shoes—one for the stage, one for everyday life. The positive impact was immediate and it gave me an idea.

Dancers often perform with injury (and we know now that those injuries are usually caused by a locked or damaged human spring). Our Wiggles cast is no different—shin splints, knee and hip problems, herniated discs that won't heal. So on our last day in Chicago before we left Dr. Stoxen behind and headed to Detroit I asked about twenty members of the cast and crew to meet me in the lobby of the House of Blues Hotel where we'd been staying.

"Today," I announced when all were assembled, "we're going shoe shopping." I admit, I got a few strange looks, especially from the crew guys, and I had to fend off several requests for Manolo Blahniks. But, eventually, after they'd all questioned my sanity, we piled into six yellow taxis and headed to a small Chicago shoe store the doctor had recommended. The store assistant was a little taken aback when we squeezed in and lined up to be fitted.

Hopefully, we didn't cost the store business with impromptu sing-alongs of Wiggles tunes. Granted, we did get some strange looks.

Eventually, with Dr. Stoxen selecting the shoes each person needed, I bought everyone two pairs. Within days people said they noticed a transformation courtesy of the shoes.

It's now mandatory for The Wiggles cast to wear appropriate footwear, and for years I bought everyone appropriate shoes at the start of each tour. The boost in the general health of the tour party has been breathtaking. Since employing chiropractors in addition to a masseur backstage and taking care to ensure footwear is correctly fitted, we haven't had a serious injury.

. . . .

Shoe Rules

Always seek out experienced shoe salespeople to help select and fit footwear. Here are a few things experts should know and you should be aware of:

- Shoes should stabilize and support the heel (in the safe range between supination and pronation).
- Ensure the width of the heel is measured in the process of fitting—not just the length of the foot.
- The heel cups, or "counters," should be strong and durable, and there should be no space between the heel and the counter. They should fit snugly.
- Don't ask for arch supports. If the heel is accommodated correctly, the spring in the arch is all the help the foot needs.
- Buy water-resistant shoes so the leather doesn't soften. Also, the footwear should "breathe," allowing perspiration to dissipate.
- Buy two pairs of the same style rather than wearing the same shoes every day.

- Weigh the shoes before purchasing them. Aim for 14 ounces, which is appropriate for most people, or 10 ounces if you have small feet. Remember: a few extra ounces means your feet are lifting hundreds of additional pounds over the course of taking the 10,000 steps we take every day—it's like dragging around an additional 1,250 pounds daily.

- Minimize the variety of styles you wear. Each style affects your movement patterns. Having to adapt often leads to bad habits.

- Don't buy brands on reputation alone (or because they just look good). Evaluate each pair for its ability to provide healthy stress-free and springy motion to the feet.

- Remember—your shoe size changes with changes in weight, age, and exercise routines, so check your fitting every time you purchase new shoes.

- Many athletic shoes have high heels built in. Do not get a shoe with a one-inch heel.

· ·

The great footwear irony is that you start wearing shoes because you think they will protect your feet when in fact they are the reason you'll eventually feel—or are being be told by a doctor (other than Anti-Shoe Doctor)—that you need lifelong therapy, arch supports or orthotics, surgical boots, or braces.

The current standard of care dictates that if you have a problem with your feet, you add layer upon layer of artificial support rather than correcting the issue by unlocking the spring and strengthening the muscles supporting it (naturally). I'm not qualified to tell you to do much of anything, except maybe read to your kids more. Having said that, it's worth having full knowledge, courtesy of Dr. Stoxen, about what those supports actually do to you.

Many put supports under the arch, which basically locks the spring (its compression/elastic deformity and rebound). The spring is already suspended from above by muscles; it doesn't need its path blocked by something. Some orthotics jam the foot spring inside the shoe; they also shift the body and limit spring loading and shock absorption. They do nothing to strengthen the weak muscles that support the foot. It's not unlike wearing a girdle. Instead of doing exercises to develop the muscles of your abs you pour yourself into a girdle, which—like an ill-fitting orthotic—won't allow your body to become stronger, making it the weakest link in your musculoskeletal linkage system.

Nice Toes

The analysis of your walking pattern we did in the mirror provides a good list of the potential flaws and bad habits we've developed in our stride, as well as providing a guide to whether and where a locked spring mechanism is impacting us.

But there are two more crucial observations we need to make as we move this discussion toward strengthening the human spring—the first through resistance routines, then impact exercises (supercharging).

A study at Harvard University in January 2010 (Lieberman et al., published in *Nature* magazine) reinforced much of what Dr. Stoxen told me back in 2004 about both my spring and the potential benefit of exercising in bare feet. In part it focused on how we bring our foot into contact with the ground when we run. Are we heel first, do we land midfoot, or maybe with the forefoot?

According to Dr. Stoxen, landing on the heel is illadvised because the *spring engineering* in that part of the foot is inadequate for the task of absorbing the shock of impact. Also, the heel landing doesn't make good use of the spring in the foot arch, ensuring the force of the collision with the ground just rattles through your bones. The doctor refers to this as a decelerated landing. This was my landing when I first met Dr Stoxen. The impact was such a "bang," my calf muscle literally shook when I planted my foot down. If your body mass is coming down behind the heel, you are getting minimal help from your spring mechanism and failing to make use of gravity's pull to boost you along.

On the other hand, if you're landing on the midfoot or forefoot, and your center of gravity is over the top of your arch spring (neutral landing), you get the benefit of the spring being able to load the force efficiently then release it to propel you forward.

What's more, if your body mass lands forward of the foot it becomes an accelerated landing because the stress of the landing is absorbed into the ideal area of the spring and released to energize forward movement.

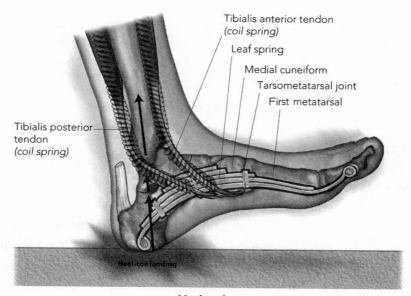

Heel strike.

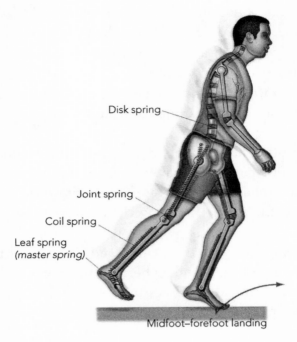

Disk spring

Joint spring

Coil spring

Leaf spring
(master spring)

Midfoot–forefoot landing

Spring walking; note the accelerated landing.

In a sense you are in a controlled fall with gravity hauling you forward, making walking or running much more efficient.

Thus, heel strikes: Not good.

Neutral or accelerated landing: Good.

So come on outside in the sun for a minute—no, don't worry, I'm not going to make you run . . . yet . . . we're going to take a leisurely walk and talk about our kids and maybe our mutual relatives from a million years or so ago, while we observe what kind of landing your foot is making with each step.

We're looking for heel strikes and one other common motion problem: the sweep gait. Instead of pointing that second toe in the direction you're going, a locked arch spring sends the foot off in a sweeping movement to the side. The foot can't spring forward so it does a little semicircle to advance rather than moving in a linear fashion to the next impact.

Now, get the kids and grandma out here; they can do this, too, and it's always helpful to have extra sets of eyes on the landings.

One of the problems in accurately observing your own gait is that you've grown familiar with the way you walk. It just looks *normal*, even if it isn't, especially in footwear. I was oblivious to my heel striking, not only because I was uninformed about the mechanics of movement, but due to the cushioned shoes I was accustomed to wearing over the last several decades. Sneakers and the high-tech shoes that, we are emphatically told, improve "performance" actually mask the devastating impact heel strikes can make over time.

Over 30 years you take about 100 million steps. That's a lot of practice at walking the wrong way. Even subtle abnormal foot strikes can eventually wear down joints to the bones, Dr. Stoxen said. But for years I was blissfully unaware of the bad habits I perpetuated in my cushioned sneakers. Of course that was before the Anti-Shoe Doctor got to me and let me know I was disrespecting Hooke's Law.

"They're just sneakers," I said meekly. "And who's this Hooke fellow?"

Whoops, I opened the door there to a little physics discussion—I should have remained silent! The law is named after Robert Hooke, a seventeenth-century British physicist (so he's slightly older than Fatty). It states that the extension of a spring is in direct proportion to the load applied to it.

Meaning what, in terms of my colorful sneakers, Doc?

"The deeper a spring depresses, the more energy it recycles back to the mechanism," he said. "Your sneakers—any shoes—as binding devices restrict the foot and don't allow the spring to depress as deeply as it would. Over time, the spring stiffens with scar tissue and deforms its shape more and more—it's like pouring glue on a spring. Furthermore, they don't exercise the arch mechanism to capacity so it won't become more elastic and return even more energy to the body."

Seems modern footwear, in some ways, isn't so different from the extreme, thousand-year-old foot binding practices in some cultures that resulted in complete and rapid devastation of the feet. At the very least, contemporary shoe styles marketed at women often make the foot thinner, taking away the toes' capacity to spread on landing to assist with balance. Similarly, men's pointy shoes induce scar tissue, making the foot less pliable and thus less able to absorb landings.

Also, the stiffer the joints in the foot, the harder it is for the muscles to adjust in assisting with balance. This is often why older people fall.

"It's not natural," he said, noting babies have the right idea as they drive their mothers nuts kicking off their shoes all the time.

So, gentle reader, in honor of Mr. Hooke and babies everywhere, let's shed our shoes again and, while trying to avoid heel strikes and keeping an eye out for that rogue sweeping gait, walk. (Remember the other flaws identified in our walk analysis, too.)

Yes, that's the first step in this revolutionary program of strengthening and supercharging—teaching yourself healthy walking. In the backyard, down the road, around the house, wherever. Don't be concerned, we'll be back inside soon, doing resistance exercises to strengthen your spring mechanism. If we're successful, maybe, on down the road, this little wander might evolve into a cross-country jog in bare feet. But for the moment, enjoy the feel of the earth beneath your feet and make a little statement in a world that's getting flatter and fatter for most people.

Many of us are overweight and sedentary, so going for a walk, including a hill or two, is a pretty good idea, anytime. Uneven terrain helps our bodies adapt. The muscles supporting the arch are stimulated when the foot is in a nonflat position.

A few hundred thousand years ago, our ancestors didn't only move in a straight line over flat terrain when they had to nab a meal for the family. Chasing those critters was hard work—

dashing one way and another over torrid landscapes. And, as far as we can tell, they weren't wearing basketball shoes or runners! In fact, millions of our brothers and sisters—many in emerging nations—walk and run with bare feet or minimal footwear today. Not surprisingly, the prevalence of human spring–related illness or injury in those communities is far less than in many advanced cultures.

Our own kids with their yet to be damaged human springs often benefit from barefoot excursions. We noted earlier how kids rebound (like springs) from falls or tumbles that would likely incapacitate many adults. They've got the edge not only because their spring mechanism doesn't tend to lock up as readily as ours, but they are exercising and strengthening the master spring every day as they zig-zag playing tag or haul themselves up a backyard tree or simply walk in circles for no apparent reason.

I realize the pressure is on to ensure people know your kid is wellcared for and as wellattired as his or her peers. But do your little ones a favor and hide their shoes as often as possible, or at least set aside some time when barefoot play (indoors and outdoors) is compulsory, before they pick up the computer game console or the television remote.

Simply making a rule barring shoes in the house helps the cause for adults and children. As you politely request the next visitor to your home takes off their enormous boots and leaves them at the door, you can confidently assert that your concern is not for the priceless Persian rugs on the floor, but the integrity of the guest's human spring. Go on, be brave.

6

Work It Out

I'm not a gym guy.

I've always loved sports and outdoor activities but the idea of being in a room surrounded by machinery, weights, and grunting people strikes me as being a little similar to being in prison. So when it came to Dr. Stoxen explaining and demonstrating the concept of strengthening and charging the spring to me, I was thinking I was about to do "time."

But, hey, it wouldn't be so bad. I'd get myself a trainer who would give me appropriate foot and ankle exercises and help me with my other spring issues and I'd gradually become a regular gym junkie.

Um, what are you laughing at, Doc?

"Have you ever seen anyone at your local gym exercising the foot arch?"

Well, no . . .

"Have you ever seen anyone exercising at a gym in bare feet?"

Oh, I guess not. In fact, I'm pretty sure that's banned in most gyms.

"Correct. It's even compulsory for most schoolchildren in the United States to wear sneakers during gym class," he said. "Martial artists don't wear shoes and seem to cope pretty well. And gymnasts land on bare feet all the time. Why is that so different from kids running around in bare feet?" He also pointed out that it's odd we are encouraged not to bind body parts during workouts so they can get the full benefit of the conditioning, yet are forced to wear restrictive shoes.

It's not only the traditional medical community that fails to see the body as a completely integrated system; even those in the business of fitness tend to overlook the most crucial part of the human system, the foundation.

Dr. Stoxen has an extensive background not only in rehabilitating but in training world-class athletes, including a host of national and world champions. Recently inducted into the National Fitness Hall of Fame, he's worked with many of the greats in the workout world and understands the desire of some to sculpt and hone their bodies.

His close association with the bodybuilding community, including a long stint as a member of the editorial advisory board for Joe Weider's *Muscle and Fitness* magazine, has helped him appreciate the dedication many of these athletes exercise daily.

"People want to develop their bodies by resistance exercise," he said. "They work on the muscles in the leg—the calves—hip, chest, and back.

"Fantastic workout examples like Charles Atlas, Joe Weider, and Arnold Schwarzenegger: They sculpt and strengthen every part of their body—above the ankle."

And there's the rub, as none of the muscles they spend countless hours developing directly support the master spring in the human mechanism, "which you need to run or simply walk." Subsequently most of those strong guys who pile on 40 pounds of muscle without working their spring mechanism are just like the

rest of us—accidents waiting to happen. (Think, too, about pregnant moms. They add 40 pounds, and in the third trimester swap
support shoes for loose-fitting footwear as their feet swell. It's no
wonder they hurt all over in that last three months.)

On the sports field, watch the athletes warm up and stretch
their hamstrings before bounding onto the field, or prep for a con-
test by "loosening up"—their arms, neck, shoulders, hips, and calves
. . . but the humble foot? If it's lucky, it might get a bit of a shake.

Keep in mind the foot, or specifically the arch spring, is absorbing enormous force. As you walk you impose one to two times
your body weight worth of force on the spring system. That is like
jogging three to four times, running four to five, and plyometrics
exercise up to ten times.

For a 180-pound man running in a race, that equates to
roughly 540 to 900 lbs. of force with every step. That is, you're
expecting your spring to process tens of thousands of pounds of
force in the course of exercising. Unfortunately, the vast majority
of even the best athletes do little or nothing to ensure that the
muscles and joints around the foundation of our bodies are in
good shape. (Just as an aside, is it any wonder ankle strains, sprains,
and fractures are among the most common sports injuries?)

This is also a graphic reminder of how devastating doing any
sort of exercise on a locked spring can be, so before attempting
any of the routines we'll be discussing next, remember to stretch
and ensure your spring is unlocked.

It's a Pirate Party

My friend Paul Paddick has been with The Wiggles full-time since
1994. As Captain Feathersword, the friendly pirate, he's indispen-
sible, having made that character something extraspecial in our
show on stage, television, and DVD.

Paddy has stuck with us, even though he's a classically trained
singer and actor who will one day again, no doubt, shine as a

dramatic performer. He was a rising star in Australian musical theater when we *kidnapped* him.

Over the years, I know he's been conflicted occasionally about focusing his talents on just one performance genre. At one stage, I thought we were going to lose him, and as fate would have it he happened to run into the fine Aussie actor Hugh Jackman, who was rapidly climbing the ladder in Hollywood.

Hugh had attended the same drama school as Paddy (the Western Australia Academy of Performing Arts) and it would have been hard for my friend not to look at his fellow thespian and think "what could have been." But before Paddy could get the lowdown on the rising star, Jackman cornered him and enthused: "Man, you're in The Wiggles. You're Captain Feathersword, that's incredible!" And for that praise, which helped solidify Paddy's resolve to stay with us, we'll be forever grateful.

Paddy didn't actually start off as Captain Feathersword. His first role was as a stand in for me in 1993 when, you guessed it, I was knocked out of action by an injury (hernia). Fresh from starring in a national production of *West Side Story*, Paddy found himself in the somewhat otherworldly circumstance of traveling in the dead of night through rural Australia in a minivan with my bandmates.

Fatty was driving, of course. He headed down an ink-black back road toward the town of Mudgee in New South Wales when, without warning, "he stops the car in the middle of nowhere and switches off the lights," Paddy recalled. "It's pitch black and I'm wondering what's going on and suddenly the music from *Psycho* comes blasting out." Paddy passed his initiation with only a few emotional scars and went on to travel Australia and the world with us countless times.

When you're on the road for so long, you develop a few good and, in my case, many bad habits. Paddy, by contrast, has always looked after himself by setting up routines to preserve his physical health and sanity. Chief among them is his *in-room* workout.

Take your average hotel room with a couple of chairs, a desk or table, and a few heavy vases or appliances and Paddy makes it a gym. Using his own body weight and the furniture as props he gradually developed his own unique fitness and strengthening program, incorporating a variety of original exercises.

The simplest part of the routine is doing push-ups against an elevated prop (a chair or a low table), so he works multiple parts of the body and tests lower-body balance. He uses various pieces of furniture to make demands on different muscle groups. Keeping toes on the ground and the back straight while pushing up on a strong, high chair, for example, works not only the shoulders and arms but the abs and the lower back. I was always amazed at how effective his self-designed program seemed to be. He started off doing relatively easy exercises and gradually and consistently made them more challenging. As a result Paddy built muscle and mass very swiftly—you could almost see him bulking up over just a few days.

I've come to learn now that what he was doing was a classic case of positive adaptation, and that concept is central to successfully strengthening and "charging" the muscles supporting the human spring.

Adaptation

Why do we exercise?

The endorphin release is reason enough. It might not be the first thing you notice when you're taking deep breaths and sweating profusely, but try going without exercise for a while and notice how your mood changes. Getting out and doing a bit of exercise helps reduce stress, makes you look better, and is a great way to improve the quality of your sleep (yes, even mine).

It might sound obvious, but it can never be said enough: If you pass up the chance to exercise you start to lose muscle and your heart and lungs have to work harder to do basic tasks.

The biggest mistake people make when they start an exercise program is that they exert themselves while their spring mechanism is locked. They also, almost inevitably, try to do too much too soon. The next big boo-boo is stopping and starting the campaign. Thus the message is to free your spring mechanism, start slowly, build gradually, and don't stop. Not bad advice for life generally, but I digress.

Being consistent and making the challenges incrementally more challenging provide the best value for your exercising buck. And that's what Paddy did. He did his program just about every day and very slowly he made the routines harder and harder. Eventually he reached a point where his muscles were being stretched and stressed, though not beyond the "breaking point." That's when he was exercising to his capacity and his shape seemed to change so rapidly.

As Professor Thomas D. Fahey of California State University wrote in 1998, "the body will adapt to the stress of exercise with increased fitness if the stress is above a minimum, threshold intensity. The purpose of physical training is to stress systematically the body so it improves its capacity to exercise. Physical training is beneficial only as long as it forces the body to adapt to the stress of physical effort. If the stress is not sufficient to overload the body then no adaptation occurs."

Basically muscles will get bigger and stronger if they're forced to contract at near-maximum tension (under healthy stress). This is particularly relevant, Dr. Stoxen explained, when conditioning the human spring mechanism.

One significant difference between the human spring and a mechanical spring is ours can adapt—can change when stress is applied. Positive adaptation means it gets stronger under this stress. Negative adaptation means it gets weaker without stress being applied or when the stress is derived from abnormal motion.

The goal when strengthening the spring (once it's unlocked) is to use resistance exercises to develop positive adaptation. When it comes to the next step—supercharging the spring—impact routines (running, jumping, plyometrics training) are the tools to generate positive adaptation.

One more important consideration in this process is footwear—binding devices prevent positive adaptation in the master spring. Think back to Hooke's Law as it applies to your foot. Shoes prevent the arch spring from being depressed to its capacity and so restrict the level of energy being recycled with every step. The spring is not being pushed to the maximum. The stress being applied is not above the minimum threshold intensity; subsequently, shoes induce negative adaptation on the arch spring.

Do you wear braces and girdles on other body parts when you exercise? Probably not. As gym instructors will tell you, they are binding devices that restrict movement and undercut the value of the workout. With that in mind, please dispense with shoes while we're strengthening and charging your spring.

Building Resistance

Many veteran athletes end up having back, hip, and knee replacement surgeries. Traditionally the wear and tear is explained away as being part and parcel of the physicality of their sport. But that ignores the fact that, in many cases, these champions have gone to extreme lengths to try to make their bodies more resistant to injury. They've trained religiously, been dedicated to good nutrition, and usually followed carefully constructed recovery programs. In many respects they are the *last* people who should be shackled by injury.

Dr. Stoxen often works with current and former sports legends, sometimes being called in after their surgeries have failed to improve their quality of life. Quite often both they and their doctors are confused about how they got into a deteriorated state and are searching for answers as to why surgery has failed them. Almost inevitably he finds they have severely locked spring mechanisms in the vicinity of where they had surgery and around joints that have been worn to the bone.

If only, in the course of years of dedicated training decades before, they'd worked to unlock and strengthen their springs.

Bones will still be shattered in contact sport and ankles will occasionally twist as we run, but if two athletes line up together and one has a locked spring mechanism, not only would you tip the opponent to win the race, but it's pretty clear who is more likely to end up bedridden in the future.

Using resistance to bolster the muscle support system of the human spring and improve balance not only boosts performance, it is a key ingredient in ensuring longevity whether you're an athlete, an insurance salesperson, a doctor, or a teacher. This process is not designed to convert you into a bodybuilder, a weight lifter, a gym junkie, or a gymnast. You don't have to commit to wearing Lycra outfits, leg warmers, and sweat bands or buy incredibly expensive equipment. You won't suddenly be required to pay attention to the latest health trends, consume ghastly egg and vegetable beverages, and do 20 push-ups every time you prepare to leave the house (although that's all good, so knock yourself out if you want to).

You will be required to commit to doing this program regularly—no, there's nothing to sign—just have a chat with your conscience: It's no good starting and stopping. Stay the course.

These exercises will improve the way you look and feel, but they aren't pure *vanity* routines. You won't bulk up. What we're working on primarily are the slender, neglected muscles that lie under the gastroc (the conspicuous calf muscle), the soleus (not as visible, in the lower leg), and others that strengthen the support mechanism of all seven floors of the human spring.

Shapely, toned legs are a happy byproduct of these drills that strengthen the spring linkage from toe to head. They will get stronger; you will burn calories, lose weight, and improve your spring, impact resistance, and efficiency of movement. These muscles also help pump blood back to the heart so they blast the deoxygenated and oxygenated nutrient-rich blood through the circulatory system to the cells, boosting the metabolism dramatically. Working the calf muscles heats the body quickly and makes you sweat quite profusely.

If you already work out, do these exercises before your current routine, or replace it with this one. It is that comprehensive.

Not only does stretching and strengthening your foundation provide added protection when you engage in other exertions, it generates an energy boost that makes doing your regular routine just a little easier.

If you don't yet have an exercise regimen, here's the only one you need.

Strengthening

Dr. Stoxen has also developed a specific program for spring strengthening that can be performed in a gym or at home using a few pieces of equipment. He'll detail a few specifics of that program, too.

But first I'll ask him to outline what he did for me, given the fact that I am almost always on the road, much prefer to be outdoors when I can, and often don't have access to exercise equipment. For this process of stretching and strengthening, you don't need a thing—especially shoes.

Over to you, Doc.

Back in 2004, Anthony didn't have a structured gym or exercise routine at all. He needed to lose some weight and he certainly had to find a way to work out and eat more healthfully, but he didn't know where to start.

He didn't have the time, confidence, or opportunity to go barefoot in a gym and follow choreographed drills using equipment such as pulleys, ropes, and mechanical abductors, so we had to devise a program that allowed him to strengthen his spring mechanism in a setting other than a regular workout environment.

Effectively, what we fashioned was a program that emphasizes "play"—perfect for a big kid!

None of these drills are exceptionally difficult and you can complete a session in about 15 minutes, but keep in mind you have to commit to doing them regularly—the only way to strengthen an area is to use it.

What follows is a small selection of the scores of exercises that can help strengthen your spring mechanism. It's never too early or late to initiate the program (as long as your spring is NOT locked). Start slowly, don't overdo it, and give yourself time to recover.

Do the drills in the backyard or on a strip of grass somewhere where there are no objects on the ground to hurt your feet. Maybe take the kids along and get them to do the routines with you—they're fun. If you find yourself in a playground, use the monkey bars for hanging exercises. If lifting your entire body weight off the ground is too hard to start with, practice partial suspension from a bar (keep a foot on the ground or lean on something).

What we're doing here is walking and moving gently to strengthen the suspension support mechanism before moving on to the next stage—supercharging.

So just how does that help us achieve desired results?

It's a simple application of Newtonian physics. That is, we use your body weight and acceleration to create a force in landing that the spring must resist. By doing so, it is strengthened.

Think of it this way. Say you're 150 pounds. Standing on two legs you exert a force of 75 pounds on each limb.

However, when you move, acceleration has to be added to the equation.

Thus the equation to calculate the force being resisted by your human spring is: $F = M \times A$—force equals mass (what you weigh) multiplied by acceleration (speed of movement). So the faster you move, the more force is exerted.

As Anthony outlined earlier, when you walk the force is about one to two times your body weight, and when you run it's three to five times. Plyometrics—those impact exercises—can be even greater.

To strengthen your unlocked spring mechanism we are going to initially focus on creating resistance through using your body weight to generate relatively low levels of force.

The drills concentrate on moving in multiple directions (side to side, zig-zagging, circles) to challenge spring suspension system muscles that often become weak because we don't vary our movement. We move in a straight line too much—on a flat footpath, a treadmill, or a Stairmaster—and by doing so only exercise the foot spring suspension muscles in the front and back, not on the side and elsewhere.

The number of repetitions will vary with your fitness level. Try starting with five per drill and increase gradually if you feel comfortable.

Foot and Ankle Roll
Stand with your feet shoulder width apart.
You're going to massage the ground alternately with the outside and inside edge of the feet. Use your body weight to bear down on one side for several reps, then shift to the other.

Lateral Lunge
Stand straight with your arms at your side. While anchoring with one leg, lunge laterally with the other, pushing off the

anchored ankle and foot and spreading your arms to mimic the movement of your legs. Hold the position briefly before resuming the start position and repeating. After several repetitions to one side, change the anchor leg to train the muscles on the other side.

8-Way Lunge

Stand with back straight, hands on hips, feet together. Lunge straight ahead with your right foot, then bring it back. Repeat the lunges, clockwise, until you hit *6 o'clock*. Then switch to the left foot and lunge until you get to *12 o'clock*.

This exercise helps strengthen the spring mechanism on floors 1–6. It's also great for balance, coordination, and agility.

Circle Walk

Use cones to outline a circle about 12 feet in diameter. Walk the circle at a normal pace, making sure your pelvis is directly over, or in front of, your foot as it lands. As you pick up speed, lean in. Once you complete a desired number of laps in one direction, head the other way. Tighten the circle first to eight feet, then five. Ensure that you do not land your foot heel first with each step.

Figure 8 Walk

Mark out a figure 8 course, using cones, or something similar, in an area running to about 16 feet in length. Walk the course, slowly at first. Gradually increase speed, angling your body inward as you do so.

Zig-Zag Walk

Between cones or markers spread about three to five feet apart, walk in a zig-zag route, leaning inward as you pick up speed.

Abdominal Oblique Hanging

This is a key exercise to strengthen the spring support system around the pelvis and lower back.

Use portable bars, rings, or straps, or find a local playground with monkey bars or something strong to hang from.

Slowly bend your knees, then lift your pelvis so your knees are above your waist. Laterally flex your torso to the left, then back to the right by about 30 degrees.

Breathe in and out each time you move to the side. Flex each side until you can't do any more. Once your knees drop below your waist, stop.

Abdominal Oblique Hanging.

Persistence

You'll be surprised how effective these routines are. You are pinpointing areas of the body that are rarely exercised with any consistency.

Initially, tenderness in some of these underworked areas may occur, but if you experience pain you should stop and go through the spring release process, working each spot until there is no pain.

Don't resume exercising until you are sure you have completely unlocked the spring.

If you are persistent and don't stop and start the workout every week or so, it will be enough to prepare you for the next stage.

Alternatively, if you prefer or are restricted to working in a gym or therapeutic setting, there are specific exercises making use of basic equipment that can safely and effectively strengthen the spring support mechanism.

Your trainers should be able to help with these, but you will probably have to take the lead by insisting the workout is performed in bare feet (don't do the workout in shoes). Here's a selection.

Bosu Ball Foot Training
Point the big toes slightly inward (pigeon toed) as you stand up straight on the ball. Push down, it's resistance.

Shift your weight from the left side of the foot to the right, rolling the foot in and out. Now, standing up straight, push down, lifting the front of the foot and burying the heel, and then do the opposite: bury the front half of your foot into the ball and raise the heel.

One Leg Bosu Ball Balance Training
You'll probably need to hang on at first as you stand on the ball with one foot. Balance and at the same time roll your foot back and forth from eversion (outward) to inversion (inward).

Foot Adduction Cable Training
Standing, attach a cuff and cable to the foot. The cable runs away from the body.

Start in full adduction and abduct to the end of the motion without moving the shin bone. The lower leg must not move at all (no cheating!). By holding it still, the muscles in the foot are isolated.

Foot Inversion Cable Training
Attach the cuff—the cable runs across the body. Start in full eversion and invert. Don't move that shin bone.

Hip Abduction (Cam resistance)
Stand in the center of a four-way hip machine with your legs close together. Put the resistance roll (the cam) on the outside of the thigh. Make sure it is at hip height. Keep your body still.

Abduct (push out against the cam) your leg to about 30 degrees. You *must* keep your foot pointing straight ahead (if you turn the foot, you're training a different muscle). Don't stop between repetitions.

Hip Adduction (Cam resistance)
On the four-way hip machine, raise the bar and the cam so it's high enough to offer resistance. Position the cam at the hip socket. Straddle it—start abducting and adducting within a range of 30 degrees. Keep all toes pointing straight ahead.

This works the adductor muscles of the hip joint. Again, don't stop between repetitions. Hold on to the rail if you need to until you feel sufficiently balanced to let go.

Four-Way Hip Flexion
Put both arms out in front of you. Stand on one foot, the leg straight. Position your other leg under the cam at knee height and lift to 90 degrees.

Four-Way Hip Extension
Put your arms out straight. Balance on one leg. Place the leg closest to the cam on top of it—keep the limb straight. With a minimum of movement elsewhere on the body propel the cam all the way behind you—extend as far as you can while keeping the leg on the cam straight.

Rectus Abdominus Pull Downs
You can do this on a high lat–low row machine.

Attach a bar or rope to a weight on the machine. Kneel down and hold the bar directly behind your head. Your spine is fully extended and you are stretching the abs in the kneeling position.

Pull down (and forward), curling your spine with your abs. Try to get your elbows to your knees. Repeat, breathing in and out each time. Gradually add speed, but don't swing your body around. Add weight as you get stronger.

In addition to a locked arch spring, Anthony had particular issues with the muscles supporting the spring system around the lower back and pelvis, so we worked his abdominals right from the start and I visited him on tour a few weeks after we initiated the "play" routines to provide added guidance.

He was in Tampa, stuffed into a dressing room with austere décor. It's where performers spend a lot of their time and I know them well from my work with entertainers on the road.

When I arrived I suggested we should just "hang" backstage. I meant it literally. I found what was looking for—a drainpipe near the ceiling. I strapped a couple of nylon supports to the drain, hoisted myself up, and did 100 or so repetitions of a drill working the ab–pelvic suspension system.

My point was to show Anthony you could do this vital work anywhere, anytime. He tried his hand—he did two, I think. But it was a start and pretty soon he was hooked on hanging. He'll show you later in the book what he's been able to achieve by constantly challenging himself.

He gradually built spring health and flexibility by sticking to the strengthening routines and incorporating (after several weeks) the supercharging component. Let's take a look at some of the routines he made his own, but first let me outline a central difference between strengthening and using impact drills to train the human spring.

Have rings, will travel.

Small shorts are not required.

Supercharge

Dr. Stoxen continues:

> Faster, stronger, higher, is the Olympic motto.
>
> Reaching for the sky is something athletes have done for centuries. It's just a shame so many crash land.
>
> All walking, running, and movement sports—Olympic-level or otherwise—feature two fundamental stress events:
>
> 1. The Takeoff
> 2. The Landing
>
> But most training approaches concentrate on only the takeoff, looking to build muscle to ensure our mass is launched faster through the air. The athlete, and you and I for that matter, simply have to *deal* with the impact of the

landing and somehow launch again. This ignores the fact that a 10 percent increase in the launch speed results in a 30 to 50 percent increase in the force of the landing.

In short, the human spring's ability to absorb the impact (and recycle that energy for an even more efficient takeoff) is not usually maximized. In fact, it's ignored or overlooked in favor of artificial shock absorbers in shoes.

This is why when most of us try and play the sports of our youth we end up injured. Most of the damage is done on landing. By supercharging the human spring system, we tune and strengthen that landing gear through impact exercises and routines, ensuring the shock is easily absorbed and distributed throughout the seven levels of the mechanism.

The main variant in some of these drills from the strengthening exercises is speed (acceleration). We are going from walking to jogging and running (and jumping/bounding). You want to be at a stage now where your suspension system muscles are strong enough to keep your foot rolling within the safe range between supination and pronation.

Running is, in fact, a series of jumps or hops as both feet leave the ground, so the suspension system must be primed for the much greater force of the landing.

When you run, keep in mind a few crucial rules for healthy movement:

1. Keep the second toe pointing toward the target.
2. Totally relax the foot and rest on the spring on impact so there is maximum loading of the force on impact.
3. Maintain the center of your pelvis or center of gravity just ahead of where your spring (foot) impacts the ground (for an accelerated spring landing/takeoff).

Anthony hanging backstage.

Anthony gets some help from Dr. Stoxen.

Anthony between Wiggles shows in 2007.

4. When changing directions, lead with your head and
   upper body, throwing them into a controlled "fall"
   in the direction you're headed, so you can take
   advantage of gravity.

Some of these routines repeat the strengthening
techniques but add speed and impact. Remember to land
on your midfoot or forefoot and *spring* off the ground; don't
bang your foot down in the landing/takeoff. You'll be
surprised how aerobically challenging these drills are. Our
bodies are simply not accustomed to moving this way.

Anthony started off doing just a few minutes at a time,
usually after walking through drills. Then after a few weeks,
he picked up the pace, aiming to go as fast as he could
without falling over.

Warm up and stretch beforehand. Challenge the kids to time trials (don't be surprised if they beat you—they already have fully intact, supercharged springs).

Figure 8 Runs

In a 16-foot, figure 8 circle, walk before gradually increasing speed, angling your body inside the circle as you do so. Tighten the circle to 12 feet or even six and try to maintain speed.

Circle Jog, Run, Sprint

Lean in as you jog steadily around the circle markers. Accelerate to a run and finally a sprint, leaning further in the faster you move. This accentuates the angle of the foot landing, stressing the spring suspension muscle group.

Zig-Zag Run

Between cones or markers spread about three feet apart, run in a zig-zag pattern, always leaning in the direction you're going. Don't plant your foot to change directions, rather, move your head and upper body, angling them to the target. When you body mass heads in the new direction, gravity pulls you in a controlled fall (thus your feet and spring are always behind the mass).

High Skip—Vertical and Horizontal

As you skip rhythmically, concentrate on lifting each leg, bent at the knee at the highest possible point. Use your arms to pump through the routine. When the left leg lifts, the right arm should lead and vice versa.

When you're doing a vertical skip don't think about speed, concentrate on height. A horizontal skip switches that priority (think speed, not height).

Double-Leg Lateral Hop

Stand with your feet about a shoulder-width apart; bend your knees before dropping into a squat while leaning in the direction you want to jump.

Explode out of the squat upward and to the side, swinging your arms upward as you do. As you land make sure it's on your midfoot and forefoot. Don't let the heel touch the ground until you come to a stop.

8-Point Step, Lunge, Hop or Bound

Set up four cones or markers in a row. Between each two, identify eight different spots. Stand between the cones and jump to and from the spots in front, behind, and to the side of you. Land on your midfoot, not your heels.

Side Shuffle

Stand with your feet slightly wider than a shoulder-width apart and bend your arms at the side. Slide the left foot forward to the right, then step to the right with the right foot. Keep your shoulders over your knees.

Change speed and direction for fresh challenges.

Jumping Jacks

An old favorite. Ensure you go through the full range of motion, pushing your legs up and out and fully extending your arms upward.

Lateral Cone Jumps

From side to side, jump over three or four markers, keeping your legs together and throwing your arms upward. Strive for maximum height and concentrate on landing on your midfoot or forefoot. Don't rest between jumps.

Form Is Function

Have you ever seen those heroic scenes of elite marathon runners willing themselves over the finish line? In some of the most bizarre cases, they can barely walk or they stumble all over the track, seemingly unable to control their legs.

That's an extreme example of losing form. Put simply, by holding our form, we perform the actions and movements that best serve our biomechanics, allowing for peak performance. In supercharging the spring, it's essential to maintain good form throughout the workout. Try to recognize when things are starting to slip.

When you start to lose form—maybe your arms start to hang lower, or your shoulders slump, or your feet drag—your level of functioning deteriorates. This loss of form can not only lead to an immediate injury, it delivers a damaging message to your brain. When you repeat a task over and over, such as walking or running, your brain stores that routine as memory. Burning perfect form into the memory is what helps athletes perform at the highest level without actually having to think about it. If you walk correctly, it becomes second nature to you. But your brain is only too willing to replace one memory with another, so if you start to lose form that will quickly become the routine your brain will compel you to follow.

It's like when you ride a bike: Cycle for an hour or so and when you get off and walk you'll probably experience a little unsteadiness. That's because your brain has started to replace the memory of walking with cycling, as if it's the new way you want to move. It's also why you should avoid using treadmills, stair climbers, and the like—they create patterns of motion that have the potential to replace healthy walking.

Most injuries happen when we lose form, potentially compromising the human spring.

Barefoot and Lovin' It

Even when I was tied up in knots physically and enduring regular bouts of illness, the competitive sports gene I inherited, no doubt from my father, kept pushing me to get out and play games.

There were times when I literally couldn't walk well enough to contemplate the opportunity to run after a ball or beat Fatty in a bicycle race, but if I was upright, there was a chance.

My love of cricket is abiding. It's a great game and instills the same loyalty and passions in me as I know baseball does for many in North America. Even though we had to stop playing our backstage games when many members of The Wiggles team were struggling with injury, we still managed to trot out for an occasional hit and giggle in Australia, something I was able to do regularly after Dr. Stoxen set me straight.

I used to love to test myself against the best opponents and fancied I'd had a pretty good practice partner in my brother John. John was an exceptional cricketer—a fast bowler who played at a high level in Australia and would have likely gone on to elite competition if his music career didn't get in the way.

Johnny helped me with my game to the stage where I thought I was shaping up pretty well, so when I got an invitation to play in a charity match featuring a few celebrities and some truly great Australian players I jumped at the chance. I went out to bat, bursting with confidence. I figured it would be a good test of character and technique, even though the real cricketers were obviously going easy on the rest of us. They would be thinking about me, "He's an old guy who sings and dances for kids—what would the 'Blue Wiggle' know about the finer details of this great sport?"

Little did they know, I had prepared for the game like it was an international test match, honing my skills with my brother in lengthy practice sessions. I planned to get accustomed to the conditions, play cautiously, at first against a few of the other wannabe cricketers, then dazzle the pros with my ability to thwart their best efforts.

But there was a hitch: I immediately found myself preparing to face Stuart MacGill, one of the great Australian spinners (think knuckle-ballers, North Americans: except spinners not only move the ball about in the air, they make it jump in different directions off the ground, too).

I guess I should explain, at this stage, that I enjoy the competitive banter between competitive sports people in the heat of battle. In Australia, we sometimes call it sledging.

So when I managed to handle MacGill's first few offerings fairly easily, I welcomed a little good-natured sledging from the opposition. The next ball I stroked away with belligerence and a bit of a flourish.

Ha! I had his measure. One of the great Australian players and he can't get it by me.

I couldn't resist: "Is that all you've got, MacGill?" I barked. "Come on, bring it!"

Now, MacGill is a gentleman and a good sport on and off the field, but I saw his smile dissipate about the same time I felt the blood drain from my face.

He sent the next one down. I vaguely recall the ball seemed to bobble in the air like it was being manipulated with string. "Just get the body behind the bat," I thought as it fizzed toward me. The ball hit the pitch a couple of feet in front of me and that was the last I saw of it. I was told it rocketed from left to right (a delivery known as a wrong'un) before thudding into my groin.

Well, that's one way to be put in your place.

I think the humiliation was worse than the physical pain, although later that day I endured more discomfort—from my shoes. In my embrace of barefoot exercise my feet had changed shape, basically returning to their natural slightly larger dimensions. When I tried to put my old cricket boots on that day it was quite the squeeze and by the afternoon I was seriously thinking about taking to the field sans footwear.

I completely understand why the first reaction of many people to barefoot activity is to query its safety. That's the line that's
been spun to us for years and obviously in some sports –especially
when a projectile is being thrown or launched at you—footwear
serves a protective role of sorts.

Yet, having experienced the benefits of running, jumping,
dancing—just living without footwear—it's crystal clear that we
need a change in mind-set. In a sense, wearing shoes should be the
exception, not the rule.

The Barefoot Club

I can engage in most athletic tasks without shoes. My feet don't hurt,
I have much better balance and speed, and I feel more energized.

The culprit, in many respects, is the modern running shoe,
which so many of us think is indispensable when, in fact, runners
wore a bare minimum or nothing at all on their feet before the
athletic shoe arrived on the scene in the 1970s.

Arguably the greatest of distance runners, Ethiopian Abebe
Bikila trained and raced barefoot, like many of his countrymen,
before *shoe sponsors* became a major force on the international
road and track running scene.

Dr. Stoxen has long been a great advocate of running. It is one
of the best fitness and health practices and offers a host of anti-
aging advantages. Understandably, it's a central part of many, perhaps most, fitness programs. I only run in bare feet, and though
I'm no marathoner, I can definitely see the logic of more athletes
experiencing the benefits of competing without binding devices
on their feet.

Indeed, the Anti-Shoe Doctor became the Barefoot Running
Doctor in recent years. In 2010, aged 48, Dr. Stoxen decided to
take up road running in bare feet.

Even though I am a fully paid up member of the "barefoot
club" and understand the overwhelming advantages of training

and walking without footwear, I was curious to know how difficult a challenge it would be.

"Why are you running long distances in bare feet?" I asked.

"Why are you walking with a binding device on your spring mechanism?" he countered.

Touché.

I guess it's a matter of walking the walk, and as the doctor explained, it's a commitment to demonstrating we don't have to tumble irrevocably down that path of physical deterioration, caught in the relentless march of accelerated aging.

As kids we go from barefoot to wearing shoes, then as we weaken and damage the spring we get an orthopedic appliance like an arch support—we know what damage they can do—so it's on to an orthopedic shoe, a cane, a walker, and finally, we're bedridden.

Few if any of the people using a cane to walk today would have thought when they were in their 30s or 40s that they'd end up that way. But that's the journey traditional care takes us on. By providing *supports* instead of rehabilitating the spring, the process robs us of the positive adaptation needed to make us stronger.

We've all seen family and friends succumb to this. In retrospect, I was well along that barefoot to bedridden path before my "intervention" and I'm sure you can locate yourself somewhere along that track, too.

"I wanted to reverse that process—to train so I could run barefooted again like I did as a child," Dr. Stoxen said.

So he did: training and running 300 miles, including several races, on concrete in one summer with no joint issues and a marked improvement in health.

"Actually my foot size went from 8.5 to 9.5 in three months," he said. "I was always a 9.5 but after decades of wearing constricting shoes my foot was squeezed to a smaller and stiffer 8.5."

With careful and gradual preparation, barefoot running (on a healthy human spring) boasts the same benefits as other sans shoes activities. "It's the final step in reclaiming your youth," according to Dr. Stoxen.

For many decades the footwear industry has trumpeted claims about its products providing "impact resistance and support," but as we've already discussed, shoes prevent the foot from doing the job it was designed to do and contribute extensively to the weakening and breakdown in the human spring mechanism.

Remember our conclusions on how we land on our feet: heel strikes, bad; midfoot and forefoot strikes, good?

I know that since deciding seven years ago to shed shoes every time I exercise (or am at home), I now unquestionably land on my forefoot and midfoot.

The 2010 Harvard study (Lieberman et al.) into the biomechanics of foot strikes not only found that most runners in standard running shoes heel strike, it also concluded that humans are able to run comfortably and safely barefoot or in minimal footwear by landing with a midfoot or forefoot strike. The research revealed most barefoot runners land on their forefoot, an astonishingly different strike to the vast majority of runners in shoes. In doing so, they absorb impact forces that are seven times less than heel strikers do.

Every time the concept of barefoot exercise and running is raised, there is a loud chorus of opposition banging the same drum they've been striking since the 1970s. There are also howls from sections of the medical community warning of the folly of shedding the *support* of shoes on hard surfaces.

But as the Lieberman study found, and I have demonstrated, you can run barefoot on the hardest surfaces without any discomfort.

Gradual Change

No one is saying to whip off your running shoes and take to the streets in bare feet immediately. As we've shown time and again in these pages, the best advice and the most insightful knowledge is common sense.

If you plan to move toward running without shoes, start on grass and move to harder surfaces slowly. Before each session spend at least 30 minutes prepping your feet with stretching and massaging the arches, ankles, calves, outer thighs, hips, and back. If you feel tender spots when running, stop and plant your thumb into the area of concern, maintaining constant pressure until the ache goes away.

Once you start venturing out, get someone to film you to ensure you're not heel landing or overpronating. If you are, go back to the strengthening and supercharging routines before trying again. When you're comfortable, occasionally run in zigzag patterns to strengthen the spring suspension system, but be careful not to overdo it.

Avoid running distances that fully test your staying capacity. Remember that when you tire, that's when you lose form. Proper alignment is harder to maintain and the foot landing could be compromised.

See you on the street.

7

Get Your Motor Running

We were a pretty happy bunch in 2005, although as my fitness and health improved, courtesy of the treatment from Dr. Stoxen and a workout plan embraced by a bunch of cast members, Pagey seemed to be cracking up a bit with injury and illness.

But overall, things were coming together in ways I could not have dreamed a few months before. I was reveling in a change of lifestyle and, for the first time in ages, got to enjoy The Wiggles' success. I wasn't up and down all the time—there was equilibrium about my world, a sensation further enhanced by the fact that Miki was pregnant again.

As another of Fatty's contemporaries, nineteenth-century writer Orison Swett Marden, said: "Work, love and play are the great balance wheels of man's being." Maintaining balance for me, especially with the influence of episodes of depression, will always be a challenge, but I had most of the elements in place again in 2005.

My main bugbear was my continuing digestive problem.

A positive offshoot of working briefly with Dr. Stoxen was a noticeable lift in my general health, including a slight improvement in my digestive system. But, as he warned me, I'd been brewing a toxic soup of inflammation for decades and that wasn't something that simply disappeared overnight. While my aches and pains had subsided markedly, I needed an intense and focused plan to turn around my big ongoing health issue. Not only was it embarrassing and debilitating personally, there were times it threatened to spill into public focus—and believe me, you wouldn't want to see that happen.

I was especially ill on the morning of a television appearance we were making in Australia after returning from one U.S. tour. We'd agreed to a rare appearance out of our Wiggles "uniforms" to discuss our success on the variety program *Rove* with host Rove McManus. Just before we were due on set, I was forced to answer "the call." I scrambled to the toilet—I'll spare you the details. I made it back, literally as McManus called us onto the stage. It was awful, and I was so distracted and humiliated I could barely think straight. Of course, my bandmates were used to it, but it didn't make it any less embarrassing.

Anyway, I was trying to focus as McManus, a very funny man and good bloke, asked about our recent movements.

Eventually he turned to Pagey and in the course of asking a question said something about us "exploding all around the world." The Yellow Wiggle, with my eleventh-hour emergency dash to the toilet fresh in his mind, couldn't contain himself and burst into a giggling fit. With Pagey unable to answer, McManus being the pro he is, shifted to addressing the next question to me. Who knows what I said.

It happened with great frequency over the years: just before shows, during shows, at dinners, functions, appearances. Enough! I'd been emboldened by my *reconstruction* in the hands of Dr. Stoxen and decided to explain my situation to another chiropractor who had come to us highly recommended during a tour of the U.S. west coast.

Dr. Richard Gringeri has a well-established practice in Santa Clara, on the doorstep of Silicon Valley, and helped us out backstage in Oakland, California. As it happens, his focus is not only chiropractic neurology, he is also a certified digestive specialist. ("There are no coincidences," as a friend of The Wiggles, psychic John Edward, likes to say.)

I outlined to him Dr. Stoxen's concerns that I had been fueling my damaged system for years with all the wrong things, including processed fast foods which, together with my general poor health, regular weight gain over the years, and stressful lifestyle, had aggravated my irritable bowel syndrome and food sensitivities.

What's more, although I was physically getting back into great shape, I still had a tendency to quickly descend into illness.

"Hmm, sounds like a lot of inflammation in your digestive system," he said, nodding knowingly. Inflammation, again? Didn't I just have an inflammation intervention with Dr. Stoxen? Of course I had, and was so much better for it, but all those years of greasy spoons—days when I felt compelled, because of exhaustion, to down numerous sugary drinks and pick-me-up fatty foods, had taken a torrid toll.

"When your body has trouble digesting food it eventually recruits white blood cells—your immune system—to help out," he explained. (It's a process called digestive leukocytosis.) "In time the immune system isn't capable of handling the additional work and your food does not get completely digested."

The food rots in the intestines and becomes toxic—nice, I know. Eventually the body gets rid of it, but by that time the toxic mess has been absorbed in the intestines and passed into the bloodstream.

"This requires the body to mount an immune-inflammatory response," Dr. Gringeri said.

And we know what that does to you.

Over the years I'd visited nutritional experts and specialists and been promised a new lease on life if I adopted new dietary guidelines and changed my lifestyle. I had followed their usually generic prescriptions and noticed a difference on occasion but it was always temporary and rarely comprehensive.

Dr. Gringeri, however, talked at length and in commonsense terms about the benefits of combining chiropractic treatment with a plan to identify the origins of my problem, develop a plan of action to treat the problem, and provide appropriate support to my digestive system, which had been ravaged by inflammation and toxicity.

"One small step at a time," he said, much to my relief.

What seemed unique to me in the Gringeri plan was the rigorous, detailed testing and evaluation of a patient's digestive situation by focusing on the functioning of the body's control center, the nervous system. He credited enzyme therapy expert Dr. Howard Loomis, chiropractic nutritionist Dr. Freddie Ulan, and chiropractic neurologist Dr. Ted Carrick as major influences in the development of his multidisciplinary approach.

Initially, as he plotted his plan, I got that feeling I had experienced seven months before with Dr. Stoxen: I could connect the dots. There was a reason for everything. There would be no stabs in the dark or "let's see how it goes." And, honestly, having witnessed what chiropractors could do, I wasn't as blind to the possibilities or as skeptical as I might have been previously.

Hey, maybe it would be possible in the future to spend less time in airline toilets and more in the company of my wife, family, and colleagues without having to rush off unexpectedly or make plans for the night that didn't revolve around the location of a restroom.

The short story is, that's what happened. When it did, I wanted to know exactly how, and the more I understood, the clearer it became that this nondrug approach is based on yet another way of looking at the human body that the health care system often ignores.

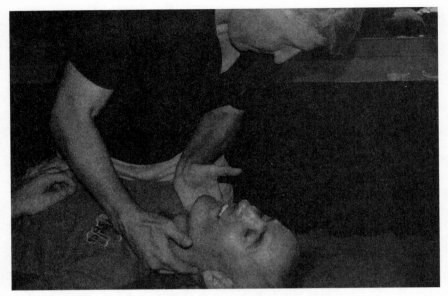

Anthony between Wiggles shows in 2007.

. . . .

Getting to Know You

You may not get the chance to visit personally with Doc Rich, but by getting an appreciation of the kind of detail he seeks in order to compile a picture of each patient's situation, you'll further appreciate why I was initially more impressed and curious about his process than that of other experts.

Importantly, the patient is an active part of the doctor's process of investigation and discovery (you know how I feel about inclusion).

Seeking to know you, literally inside out, he launches a battery of tests and surveys, piecing together your unique profile, allowing you and your metabolism to tell him, in a sense, what is wrong and what needs to be done to correct it.

In an initial consultation, Dr. Gringeri meticulously notes every symptom you've ever had and guides you through the process of outlining how long you've experienced each one: how severe they've been, what aggravated them, and what seemed to alleviate them. It's amazing, as you look back over the years of enduring discomfort, illness, or pain, to see the patterns that evolved from certain habits.

A physical examination follows. He pushes and prods up to seventy points on the body, looking for swelling, muscle spasms, and tenderness. He asks you to rate the level of discomfort on a scale of one to three—I had a few "ouch" threes.

The nutritious herbal cocktail (shaken, not stirred) he asks you to drink may not win any flavor awards, but it's the next step in the process. It's odd—you can almost feel it exploring your metabolism as it goes down.

As Dr. Gringeri waits for about forty minutes for his potion to settle, he produces an eleven-page survey. You're asked to detail what you crave and what you eat and drink. There are also about ten questions related to the functioning of each digestive organ—no lying now. It's not exactly sexy reading, but it is crucial to gaining a precise understanding of your situation.

The last step is laboratory testing of overall toxicity levels, calcium levels, and liver and kidney function. In the end, he knows more about you than most other people in your life, allowing him to devise a very specific diet and nutritional plan. If this detailed testing isn't on your agenda, at least start the process of self-evaluation by writing down the foods and beverages you crave and the impact they have on you. This is not unlike what I did years ago to keep track of the foods for which I seemed to have a sensitivity.

Making notes about additional details, such as the frequency of occurrence, symptoms (internal and external) of illness or reactions, and the length of episodes is also helpful. Also make regular diary entries about where you have pain on your body and try to keep track of when it comes and goes. In the hands of a responsible nutritionist or astute chiropractor these records should provide valuable insight.

· ·

You'll recall when we discussed Dr. Stoxen's approach I asked how many doctors routinely check your feet when you're complaining of illness or injury (above the ankles)?

Well, here's another one to ponder: When was the last time an MD wanted to evaluate your nervous system as a routine part of a consultation when you were sick?

OK, get that full-sized human specimen out here. No, no Wiggles shirt—oh, maybe a purple one, Fatty has everything functioning correctly.

So why do they teach us in second grade that the nervous system controls all the body's functions? If that is the case, surely it would be the first place to look when something goes wrong?

After all, as Dr. Gringeri explained, the body is made up of billions of cells that rely on the delivery of nutrients and oxygen and a process to get rid of waste and carbon dioxide. The delivery and the waste disposal functions are largely performed by the circulatory, respiratory, and digestive systems, which are directed and controlled by, you guessed it, the nervous system. And, like other parts of our body, the nervous system is made up of cells that require nutrients, oxygen, and activation in order to function.

Allow me to speak with the insight of a second grader: If something's messed up in there, ain't it gonna mess up the other bits, too?

Thank you, thank you, please pay the nurse at the door.

The Human Engine

Dr. Gringeri didn't realize that only seven months before I met him I had worked extremely hard to get my head around the idea I was like a building with a poor foundation. So when he told me my body was an engine, just like a car's, I probably shouldn't have moaned.

"I didn't say like an engine, the human body *is* an engine," he explained.

"In order for a car to operate it needs fuel (gas), oxygen (air that mixes with the fuel), and a spark (spark plugs). The same is true for your body: Its fuel is food, it takes in oxygen, and it needs a spark—the electrical activation comes from the nervous system."

Recalling my decades of illness and injury, I could fully comprehend the implications of blowing a fuse and it would be fair to say, even though my chassis had been totally rebuilt, I was still emitting an awful lot of black smoke.

Thus, I was prepared to run with the analogy, as long as Dr. Gringeri proved to be a better mechanic than the dodgy guy who used to service my rusty four-cylinder clunker back in the days of The Cockroaches.

"Turn me into a finely tuned Porsche, Doc," I said before catching myself, "or maybe an environmentally friendly hybrid, anything—just not Fatty's minivan—I'll leave it to you."

Dr. Gringeri had confirmed with tests that my biggest problem was my fuel intake and what happened to it. Put simply, I put a lot of bad stuff in, my body processed it poorly, and the result was a high level of toxicity and inflammation.

We'll come back to this in detail in the next chapter because there is so much to explore, but as he explained, the key is to bypass the incompetent digestive system to improve the way fuel (food) is broken down, providing much-needed nutrients to the body. To ensure the fuel is used properly in the future, a change of diet helps create better health and in the process cleanses the system.

Central to the process are the enzymes in the food you eat and those produced naturally by your body. Enzymes are responsible for all digestion and help fight conditions including inflammation, pain, and allergies. They are produced by all the cells in the body, but when cells become too toxic enzyme production stops, robbing us of our health.

Essentially Dr. Gringeri devised a plan for me based around careful nutrition and the frequent intake of enzyme and food supplements to get my system up and running again. I'll detail that in the coming pages as well as explore what enzymes and other supplements can do for your situation.

Luckily, largely due to the work I did with Dr. Stoxen, the other key components in running an engine, my *oxygen* and *spark*, were available in abundance.

However, many people have deficiencies in these areas. Fortunately, that is a situation that's both identifiable and treatable.

Oxygen

My great-grandfather Paddy Condon ran and owned the largest pub in western New South Wales, *The Great Western*, in the mining town of Cobar. It was also my dad's childhood home after his parents took over the hotel from Paddy. The story goes that Paddy, a bear of a man, used to keep his dining room open and offer free meals to the poor during the Depression. He was the head of the miners' union in Cobar, a boxing referee, and a larger-than-life character in many ways. As he aged, he got sick and, as was the practice in the day, on advice from doctors, he was moved temporarily from the hellishly hot surrounds of Cobar on the edge of the outback to the relatively cool, tree-covered region of the Blue Mountains. The belief was that the clean air and a greater oxygen intake in the mountains would help him breathe more easily and initiate a recovery.

It was a kind of environmental medication that was embraced by thousands who were battling illness or just seeking a healthier existence—my grandfather spent time there after being struck with tuberculosis. When Paddy died they put him on the lumbering train back to Cobar. They say every station along the route was packed with mourners.

Whether there is contemporary science to back up the idea that the gorgeous Blue Mountains have better air quality than gritty Cobar isn't quite the point. The fact that there has long been recognition that the amount of oxygen we take in is vital to our health is. For generations the scientific community has theorized on the impact oxygen has not just in keeping us alive, but in thwarting disease. Back in 1931, German medical doctor and scientist Otto Warburg won the Nobel Prize in Physiology for showing that cancer cannot exist in an oxygen-rich cellular environment, work that sprouted decades of investigation and debate.

There also are ongoing arguments about how the quality of the air we breathe differs from previous times—with some, like chiropractor and author Dr. James Chappell, asserting the amount of oxygen in the atmosphere has been reduced by almost 50 percent in the last 100 years. Regardless of the level of difference, there seems to be a growing belief that many, if not most of us, are oxygen deprived. Certainly your body's oxygen levels and its ability to use oxygen diminish with age, according to Dr. Gringeri.

That interferes with the vital process of oxidative phosphorylation—hydrogen combining with oxygen—which generates most of your engine's energy.

"Also, oxygen itself is fuel for the body as it mixes with food and is burned off," he said. "So when researchers attribute many age-related diseases to a lack of oxygen or decreased efficiency of oxidative phosphorylation, you can understand why."

With less energy to perform its functions, the body gets weaker and more susceptible to illness and injury. When you climb those ten stairs at home these days, you are possibly blow-ing harder than a few years ago when you used to run up.

"It's just age," I hear you say.

Well, yes and no, grandpa.

To breathe the air that contains that delicious oxygen, your rib cage must expand. That's not such a big deal for those lively kids who, you'll remember from Dr. Stoxen's observations, have pristine spring mechanisms and dart around endlessly exercising their system while taking large gulps of air in the process.

But as we age the bones and joints that make up our rib cages become less flexible, joint motion is reduced, and our oxygen intake diminishes. In turn, this further impacts joint motion as oxygen is required to maintain flexibility. Combined with the likely fact that you're not doing as much aerobic exercise (which oxygenates the blood) as you used to, you can see why your aging cells are hankering for more oxygen.

It is possible to get chiropractic treatment to assist in making your rib cage flexible again, as in your youth, and thus help your oxygen intake.

Specific chiropractic treatment can dramatically aid posture, too. I'll let Dr. Gringeri explain: "There are seven layers of muscles over the spine. The deepest few layers are referred to as the erec-tor spinae muscles, and their tone controls posture.

"That tone is determined by the activity level of a part of the brain, the cerebellum. Exercise and oxygen activate the cerebel-lum, but nothing activates it so completely as a well-delivered coupled reduction of the cervical spine (a type of neck adjustment)."

You can also work on your posture and devise a gentle work-out plan to build aerobic capacity and target the muscles that support the ribs. Be constantly aware of the benefits of developing your capacity to improve oxygen intake and make appropriate small changes in your daily routine: walk instead of taking the bus, take the stairs not the elevator, take a stroll at lunchtime, and be conscious of your posture at home and at work.

And, as they say in the classics: Remember to breathe.

Spark

No spark, no motion.

If you were a vehicle, you'd simply replace the spark plugs, but, despite what a few innovative chiropractors want us to believe, you're not a car (or a building, for that matter).

The human engine's spark comes from a network of nerves that includes the brain and spinal cord—the nervous system.

This electrical activation network fires from one nerve to next, back and forth between the brain and the body, providing the spark to activate the functions of every cell. The proper functioning of those cells is crucial to the task of keeping us alive. If you're sick, chances are something has gone wrong with one of these bodily systems:

- Respiratory system
- Circulatory system
- Reproductive system
- Immune system
- Endocrine system (hormones)
- Digestive system

Each of these is activated and works in harmony with the others under the direction of the nervous system. It's an incredible process, with the nerves of the brain connecting with different parts to deliver commands to muscles, bones, organs, glands, tissues, and the cells.

"It will function perfectly as long as there is sufficient activation of the nervous system along the nerve channels that carry signals from the body to the spinal cord and up to the brain," Dr. Gringeri said.

"Without the brain directing the communication via your nerves, which are like the brain's wiring moving throughout the body, none of these systems would function."

Just an aside: I always thought chiropractors were effective because they took pressure off nerves. While that's true in a small percent of cases, Dr. Gringeri said, for the most part "we get people well by putting pressure on nerves." Adjustments work because they cause the nerves to fire. Activating the nervous system is the key to success.

Here's an example of all the bits of the brain (technical term) and the nerves working with the body's systems. See that piece of chocolate cake on the table? Well, put it back in the refrigerator.

Now, see that apple? Right, you're going to eat that juicy fruit and I'm going to provide the running commentary, courtesy of Dr. Gringeri.

As you take a bite, in order for your digestive system to work, your brain (via the spinal cord and the nerves) is directing these functions: activation of the chewing muscles and the production and release of saliva in the mouth. It stimulates acid- and enzyme-producing cells in the stomach. Acinar (digestive juice) and beta cells (insulin) in the pancreas and digestive glands of the small intestine are instructed to release enzymes to help break down the food (the apple will be far more cooperative than the chocolate cake in this regard).

As the apple moves through the *food tube* in your body, the brain drives and coordinates muscle activity in the digestive system, where nutrients are absorbed and waste eliminated.

The brain—everyone's finest feature—has a direct connection to, and receives sensory input from, each of the glands and organs involved so the exact amount of energy is expended to achieve the intended results.

And you thought eating an apple was simple?

You can see the potential for trouble throughout the body if the nervous system is faltering or damaged. Just as clearly, a fully functional, healthy brain–nerve spark and communication process has enormous benefits for all bodily functions, not only digestion. The nervous system, simply put, sends and receives information. When communication is seamlessly efficient, optimal health is the result.

I knew there was a reason I liked chiropractors! Even before I made the connection with the healers in this book, I was instinctively aware of the positive impact a simple chiropractic adjustment could have. Adjustments and some other physical therapy measures fire up the brain, because the spine is an integral part of the bodily system that affects all others—the nervous system.

As the doctor noted, the spinal cord is an extension of the brain, so when a chiropractor is moving the vertebrae of the spine, for example, they are impacting much more than a couple of bones. "The vertebrae protect the spinal cord," Dr. Gringeri said. "The word *vertebra* means 'bone that spins' and it's the rotation of the vertebrae that compresses mechanoreceptors within the joints and causes the activation and firing of sensory nerves that travel to your brain."

If the vertebrae don't rotate properly—say, after the impact from an accident—it reduces the sensory impulses to the brain and puts your health at risk. Without appropriate brain cell activation the brain won't perform as it should and the body stops functioning as it should. Headaches, indigestion, joint pain, fatigue, insomnia, mood swings, allergies, and asthma could be the result—the whole terrible show.

Dr. Gringeri also believes a sluggish brain that hasn't been sufficiently activated also contributes to diabetes, Parkinson's disease, high blood pressure, and obesity.

In Your Best Interests

So you've got a headache, joint pain, allergies, etc. . . . . take your pick. You go to your doctor—or several doctors, for second and third opinions. I'll bet a large box of Wags the Dog's bones that they won't check your feet and they won't assess your nervous system or work your spine. I'll bet you, though I'm not a betting man, a bag full of Dorothy's roses that they will usually provide you with medication—a painkiller, maybe a course of antibiotics.

That's what happened to me for decades. As I discussed earlier, at the height of my misery I was taking pain medication so often it made me profoundly sick. They were all prescribed medications—I never took anything more than I'd been instructed to by medical experts.

I, like millions of others, was simply doing what I was told was in my best interests. I've now come to understand that in many circumstances drugs are exactly what a sick or injured person doesn't need. Many drugs numb and shut down the body's communication system that must be functioning normally for you to heal naturally.

It's not that there's an absolute right or wrong in the way medical experts treat you—your MD in the U.S. or GP in Australia is likely one of the most insightful people in the community— it's just that he or she is the *not* the only one who can guide you to better health, which is what many drug and insurance companies would have us believe.

Let's do a quick comparison between likely treatment plans for the same injury—say, carpal tunnel syndrome in the wrist—by a regular medical doctor and Dr. Gringeri. Without being presumptuous, I think it's fair to say many doctors would prescribe a painkiller, advise rest, and perhaps advocate the use of a support. In extreme cases surgery might be scheduled.

For the Human Engine Doctor approach, it's over to you, Dr. Gringeri.

I would work to optimize the three factors for your engine to run best: oxygen, fuel, and spark. I would assess the brain and central nervous system to see if there is any area that is functioning at a lower level. The cerebral cortex inhibits pain and when sufficient activation is restored, pain levels are usually reduced or eliminated.

I would use chiropractic adjustments to activate this sluggish brain area and to alleviate nerve stress or irritation in the wrist or the neck (where the nerves in the wrist originate).

I would optimize oxygen by reducing rib fixations so that the rib cage moves more efficiently and may also give the patient supplemental oxygen. I would work with the patient on diet and nutrition to make sure that—combined with oxygen—the patient is getting the best fuel possible to the ailing cells that are causing the pain.

Rather than giving pain relievers and anti-inflammatories, I'd advise the consumption of healthy fats, like those in fish oil. You can also get them as high-quality digestive supplements. These reduce pain and inflammation. An excellent nutrient like inositol also helps to relieve nerve pain." Importantly, numbing the system with painkillers negates the natural healing process—the human engine must remain active and fully functional for the carpal tunnel problem to go away.

There, I'm feeling better already.

If you're my age you'll probably know the words to a lot of terrible songs from the 1980s. You'll also possibly be starting to experience ailments such as chronic pain, headaches, fatigue, and brain fog. Be assured this is not necessarily a payback for your misspent youth. It's often simply the result of a diminished nervous system function that occurs naturally around ages 45–50.

But take heart, middle-aged comrade, you don't have to meekly accept this deterioration and you don't have to start a new round of painkillers and anti-inflammatories to cope. A healthy lifestyle and regular care from a chiropractor who—I bet you a sachet of Captain Feathersword's eye patches—will check your back and possibly your feet, can turn things around.

E-N-Z-Y-M-E-S

The litany of my restroom horror stories in these pages may have you looking at me differently next time you come to a concert or watch a DVD with your kids, but don't go thinking every time I race from stage I'm doing something unmentionable. That's because, basically, I'm cured. I am still cautious around certain foods, but I can even eat many of the things I used to be terrified of consuming and thankfully, mercifully, it's been quite a few years since I took a world lavatory tour.

As mentioned, through testing and other evaluation, Dr. Gringeri established that my major issue was an inability to break down what I put in my digestive system. Enzymes and food supplements were a big part of my turnaround, but my recovery, under the guidance of the doctor, incorporated all elements of the Human Engine Approach.

As Dr. Gringeri explained, the ability to digest food doesn't rely on just one gland, organ, or nerve bundle. The process starts in the mouth and continues into the stomach, small intestine, and large intestine. The pancreas, liver, and gallbladder are involved too, so the nervous system has to be in great shape to coordinate this effort.

Ensuring the brain is getting enough spark and oxygen through regular adjustments and lots of exercise helped me immensely. It even affected what I wanted to eat.

Dr. Gringeri said that a bit of the brain called the hypothalamus strongly influences what foods smell and taste good (to each individual), therefore influencing food cravings—the oxygen levels in the tissues play a crucial role in this.

Clearly the physical advances I made working with Dr. Stoxen improved my condition to the point where I was already meeting oxygen and spark *requirements* when I got to Dr. Gringeri. The mind boggles when I think what probably would have happened had I been tested before being rebuilt. I'm quite sure I recognize my pre-Stoxen self in most of the traits the doctor attributed to someone who is poorly oxygenated and enduring a faltering nervous system.

When considering your own situation or that of a loved one, make a brutally honest assessment of health status across a number of fronts. It is possible to be aerobically fit, mentally alert, physically balanced, and dexterous and have the digestive system from hell, just as it is possible for your body to be processing intake correctly only for you to be enduring circulatory or immunity issues.

Either way, try and consider all medical and health options, including chiropractic care, before you pop that pill.

Break It Down

We've all heard the stories of how certain fast foods loaded with preservatives will last for days, even months. That's not a big problem, unless you're eating the stuff. Preservatives alone aren't the issue: Have you ever read the list of ingredients for a simple hamburger bun?

Bottom line—a big fat bottom line—is that many of these calorie-rich, fatty foods not only pack on the pounds; they are about as digestible as some plastics. But let's not blame any one source. Even mom's home cooking might have a few things to answer for.

I'm going to hand it over to Dr. Gringeri to explain: Food has been more difficult to process healthfully ever since someone hundreds of years ago hit on the idea of cooking everything. Enzymes, the protein molecules found in all raw foods, are the things that actually digest food. But as Dr. Edward Howell, a pioneer in enzyme research, found decades ago, heating food kills enzymes, so a diet of cooked food in large quantities over time causes degenerative diseases and impacts long-term health dramatically.

Basically, the fuel being fed to cells—enzyme-deficient foods—can't be assimilated into the body.

Around the middle years of the twentieth century, Dr. Howell hypothesized that as a result of eating enzyme-deficient foods, many children put such stress on their digestive systems that they were unable to digest properly by the time they reached adulthood.

I wonder what Dr. Howell, who died at the age of 89 in 1988, would think of the contemporary fast and processed food diet? Some of the dietary practices I come across in my work in California almost defy belief, but even "normal" nutritional habits in North America are fast-tracking ill health. From 80 to 90 percent of the average American diet is cooked (and there are similar estimates elsewhere in the western world). Keep in mind, food only needs to be heated to about 120°F degrees for enzymes to die. Your body produces its own enzymes, but if your food (fuel) input is mostly cooked, it won't be able to supply enough to service the digestion process, resulting in digestive leukocytosis, which we referred to earlier.

The remnants of rotting food pollute your metabolism. The immune system—already doing work it shouldn't have to in the absence of digestive enzymes—launches an inflammatory reaction. It gradually weakens as it works in tandem with the damaged digestive system. Your body starts to crumble: allergies, aches, pains . . . all the ailments we associate with aging and inflammation.

It didn't have to be like this.

For millions of years the human body adapted to eat and digest fresh raw fruits and vegetables and even raw meats. It has only been in the last couple of thousand years that we have been eating cooked and refined foods and maybe the last hundred that we've eaten foods with added hormones, antibiotics, preservatives, and other additives to increase shelf life. Not only are they hard to digest, they compromise the immune system, which needs enzymes.

Enzymes aren't some vague concept, by the way.

Take an apple and let it drop to the ground. You'll notice the area of impact is bruised and quickly turns brown. This is because the cells that were damaged on impact released enzymes in the surrounding area and the apple started to digest itself. The result is the rotten brown spot.

Supplements

When I first consulted with Dr. Gringeri in 2005 I was still indulging in lousy dietary habits, although I was nowhere near as bad as I had been. Nevertheless, I had a long history of overconsumption of sugar.

I could blame the stress of being on the road and ignorance, but let's face it, I knew deep down I shouldn't have been sucking on sports drinks every time I came offstage, or got ready to go onstage, or prepared to leave the arena, or when I got up in the morning . . . you get the picture.

Also, my beloved espresso hits were too frequent, and in combination with years of eating cooked and processed foods I was a nutritionist's nightmare.

Dr. Gringeri said my sugar-heavy habits likely contributed to symptoms of depression, constipation, diarrhea, fatigue, muscle weakness, and brain fog. I sure had all the signs. He designed a course of action, an enzyme and food supplement regime in addition to exercising more care with my diet.

The digestive enzymes I took were mostly to assist in breaking down carbohydrates. He also gave me a supplement containing potassium, B-complex vitamins, and vitamin C since too much sugar robs the body of electrolytes. "Sugar carries other nutrients with it when it leaves the body," he said.

I also took multivitamins and multimineral tablets, although these are not like the products at the local drugstore. These are made from whole foods that also contain digestive enzymes.

Truth be told, I was a little skeptical at the time about how effective this enzyme campaign would be. That lasted a couple of days until I was completely overwhelmed by the fact that I felt not just a little better, but completely renewed.

I started telling anyone who would listen about the transformation, but was a little short on the facts about enzymes, which, I've since established, are not all the same. The body produces enzymes that are either metabolic (helping to speed up chemical reactions in glands and organs) or digestive (produced in the mouth, stomach, pancreas, and small intestine and other key areas) to help break down food.

The enzyme supplements that are available to help bolster the digestive process vary insofar as some are designed to help with protein digestion, others carbohydrates, and some with fats. They are available over the counter, but it's wise to consult an expert to ensure you buy the appropriate type and amount.

While this is not a one-size-fits-all exercise, the doctor outlined a couple of characteristics of other patients who can benefit from an enzyme regime.

People who don't digest fats well often exhibit symptoms from diabetes to rosacea. Difficult menstrual periods or infertility also may be issues.

"We supplement with a formulation that is geared toward digesting fats, possibly a fatty acid supplement to restore levels of fatty acid that are important in absorbing foods and even restoring your hormone levels," he said.

If protein digestion is a problem, patients often have to deal with watery eyes and noses, muscle and menstrual cramping, bleeding gums, and swelling of the hands and feet. An enzyme supplement rich in protease (the enzyme that digests protein) would be in order here and possibly a protein supplement or an increase in dietary protein. Dr. Gringeri noted that many Parkinson's disease sufferers have protein digestion problems (our ability to break down protein is impeded greatly in old age).

In addition to ingesting enzymes and other supplements I also followed a general nutrition improvement plan that included eating more raw foods and fewer processed and altered foods, making sure food is consumed in its most digestible form. The easier the job of digesting, the more nutrition the body extracts.

Dr. Gringeri drew on the work of naturopathic doctor and herbalist Ian Shillington for these tips:

- Chew your food. Digestion begins in the mouth, so chew thoroughly. Smaller food particles are easier to process and they will be coated with saliva, which starts digestion.

- Eat organic food as often as possible. Many modern diseases are caused by toxicity from pesticides and chemicals in food and water. Also, commercially processed meats, fish, and poultry often contain hormones and antibiotics that are hard for the body to digest.

- Sprout your grains, nuts, seeds, and beans. These foods have enzyme inhibitors. But sprout them or at least soak them for 24 hours or more before cooking or eating and you'll get their nutritional value without interfering with the digestion of other foods.

- Avoid eating white flour, white sugar products, and refined foods. All foods that have been altered from their natural state become harder to digest. White flour and white sugar have a druglike effect on the body's digestive process.

- Strive for nutrition, not just calories. Don't just eat to feel full. Try to eat nutritionally sound foods and consider taking a daily high-quality nutritional supplement made from whole foods.

- Take a fatty acid supplement. Your body needs fat. Cell membranes are made up of layers of protein and fats. These membranes let nutrition and oxygen pass into your cells, so the healthier the membranes, the better we function. However, as we get older the membranes get stiffer and don't function as well. A fatty acid supplement will help in this regard and reduce inflammation in the body.

Diabetes: Tackling a Crisis

Experiencing the complete package—better fuel, more oxygen, and greater spark—has been a revelation for me.

Just as restoring the integrity of the human spring puts a stop to accelerated aging and potentially restores the qualities of youth, the human engine approach arrests the degeneration of our metabolism and revitalizes the systems vital to our good health.

In recent years, Dr. Gringeri has honed his approach, which incorporates nutrition, neurology, and chiropractic, and enjoyed considerable success with the most challenging cases. I've viewed testimonials from people just like me who struggled for decades with digestive issues, but also from patients with Parkinson's, Crohn's disease, chronic constipation, and diabetes.

Whatever the ailment, we seem to share a few things in common—primary among them, the long-term folly of prescription medication. OK, I'm *not* saying to throw your pills away or encouraging you to turn your back on traditional methods. But let's at least consider the possibility that these drug-free alternatives (also) work.

As Dr. Gringeri asks at the diabetes seminars he gives to packed houses in California: "If you had a health problem that could be treated either naturally or with a drug, how many of you would prefer a drug?" No hands shoot up for that one. The fact is that the biggest issues can be successfully addressed without traditional medication. I'm proof, and there's a growing army of believers. Frances, one of Dr. Gringeri's patients, is among them.

For years she had stomach pain and diarrhea. Over 12 months she underwent hospital tests and took prescribed medications.

Nothing was found, but her condition deteriorated. She stopped eating foods she felt she was allergic to and eventually became afraid to eat at all, and lost 17 pounds in a month.

The diarrhea and pain were so acute she became willing to starve herself rather than risk embarrassment. She was tired all the time, and experienced memory loss, extreme abdominal pain, deteriorating eyesight, acidic bad breath, headaches, arthritis, and insomnia. She revealed her problem to the doctor during an adjustment. He tested Frances and quickly determined the specifics of her unique digestive challenges. Using the fuel/oxygen/spark approach he worked to cleanse and revitalize her *engine*.

"One by one my symptoms went away," Frances writes. "The results were amazing."

It's not just conspicuous digestive ailments that respond favorably to the process of repairing and tuning the human engine. In recent years, Dr. Gringeri has turned his attention to the mother of all digestive diseases, diabetes.

More than 220 million people worldwide have diabetes, according to the World Health Organization (WHO), and that number is expected to swell inordinately in coming years. It's estimated that in the U.S. alone, one in three children born in the year 2000 will develop diabetes at some stage in their lives.

The American Diabetes Association (ADA) says that just under 26 million people currently have diabetes in the U.S. and 79 million have prediabetes (higher than normal blood glucose levels). Much of the world is in the grip of this swelling epidemic and, tragically, more than 80 percent of diabetes deaths occur in low- and middle-income countries. WHO projects diabetes deaths will double between 2005 and 2030.

The ADA succinctly defines diabetes as "a group of diseases characterized by high blood glucose levels that result from defects in the body's ability to produce and/or use insulin."

Stick with me here, I want us to make a connection together.

Just to clarify, much of what we eat is broken down into glucose (blood sugar)—it is *fuel* for our bodies, however, this fuel can't enter the cells without insulin (a hormone produced in the pancreas). Dr. Gringeri expanded on the definition with his perspective: "Diabetes is an inability to oxidize glucose and combust fats, so it is an oxygen deficiency and digestion problem."

"Digestion, of course, is the chemical breakdown of food by enzymatic action," he said.

Do you see where I'm going here?

Insulin, in the eyes of the doctor, is not the only key player. "It's not only a problem with sugar, we can get that under control, it's about digestion," he said.

Diabetes is often referred to as a disease of the pancreas, because the pancreas produces insulin, but the primary product of that organ is actually digestive juice—digestive enzymes. "Diabetics have a problem converting food to energy," Dr. Gringeri said. "We tackle that specific issue every day by employing the elements of the Human Engine Approach: improve fuel, oxygen, and spark."

Essentially diabetics, according to the doctor, are like the rest of us suffering from digestive challenges: They're walking around with toxicity flooding their body systems.

"They've been mildly poisoned in one way or another at some stage in their lives," he said.

Subsequently the nervous system and all its cronies are stuttering to a stop. Dr. Gringeri contends the drugs used to treat diabetes suppress sugar levels but don't do anything to amend the digestive or oxygen deficiencies in the system.

"The meds actually cause more dietary distress."

In a very real sense, Dr. Gringeri, it seems to me, is building on what science knows about diabetes by bringing his view of the human engine to the medical table, rather than completely turning away from traditional viewpoints. His approach has the added attraction of being drug-free, which for many long-term diabetes sufferers in particular is something they've never even considered as an option.

"We all get herded down this path we don't want to go down, but we're told it's the only way," he said. "Over time the only thing that generally happens is diabetics' conditions deteriorate, so they receive more medications in greater amounts. It doesn't stop the deterioration."

At best, they are in a kind of "holding pattern."

Dr. Gringeri noted that many prescription medications are in fact toxic constructs sent into the body with the intention of *killing off* one reaction in order for another reaction to thrive (and hopefully lead to wellness).

"It's basically suppression of acute disease by drug poisoning," he asserted.

"For diabetics, who are already toxic, it doesn't make sense to try and fix the situation by adding more toxicity to the equation."

The health system often covers the costs of diabetes medications and traditional treatment, a help to the many middle to lower-income folks potentially facing years of hospital, doctor, and pharmacy visits. Alternative approaches generally are not covered, meaning it often comes out of the diabetic's pocket.

It's a big step to consider coughing up your hard-earned cash when there is the ongoing availability of free meds and consultation. George, a former Olympic-standard runner and diabetic, did it, after 36 years of going nowhere fast.

He writes that when he came to Dr. Gringeri he was on insulin, metformin, glyburide, desipramine, lotensin, and simvastatin for ailments ranging from diabetes to high blood pressure, high cholesterol, and joint pain.

His health and well-being had more or less collapsed. He was weak, putting on weight, required numerous eye surgeries, and had toe-joints replaced. He couldn't work his second job, had become socially isolated, and was unable to run. Remarkably, though, he clung to a dream to return to competitive racing. As a desperate measure he consulted Dr. Gringeri.

After eight months of treatment (and carefully shedding medications in consultation with doctors) he returned to training and hired a new coach. "I am 90 percent better," he writes.

Truly, you wade through some of these testimonials and you see stuff you couldn't make up. But having experienced a transformation, I know the outcomes aren't the result of some sort of magic wand being waved or wacky treatment being employed. It's all grounded in nutritional and chiropractic science. You've got to do the work and follow the treatment guidelines to get well; it's not a shortcut, that's for sure.

It's intriguing to consider what has caused the explosion in the numbers suffering from conditions such as diabetes. The authorities tell us that in addition to heredity playing a role, increasingly sedentary lifestyles and poor dietary trends—sugary drinks, eating too many carbohydrates, fats, and proteins—are major influences. There is also a widespread belief that environmental and other unidentified factors are contributing—a concept Dr. Gringeri embraces emphatically.

"We are being mildly poisoned by antibiotics, pain relievers, blood pressure medicines . . . there are more pesticides in foods, which are packed with hormones and other additives," he said.

What do I think? Well, let me tell you what I know. I was toxic and I overcame it. I worked at exercising more and eating better—great tools in prevention and healing—but that alone didn't make the big difference. I needed the nondrug treatment Dr. Gringeri provided to complete the transformation.

I know we're on a prescription drug roundabout. I got off to try something vastly different and, through insight and hard work, got better. It's a leap of faith for many of us raised to believe there is only one way to tackle health and medical concerns.

If you do want to *jump* keep your eyes open and do it with the assistance of people who truly know what they're doing.

Take things slowly. Be smart and get well.

8

The Extra Step

For quite a few years my immediate family was actually Fergus the world's fiercest mini fox terrier, his yappy sister Pasqua, and her daughter Manuella. Pepe, a dachshund, was the ring in and regular victim of Fergus's bullying. I loved my dogs, still do, much to my neighbors' distress, but Miki came along and changed everything (except Fergus's behavior).

It was a family moment about seven years ago that, in retrospect, probably sent me off on this little health and fitness mission—it's certainly what has motivated me in recent years to strive to be as fit and strong as possible.

In addition to being exasperated with feeling ill all the time, I was made only too aware of my physical deterioration one day when Miki got home having done a spot of shopping. She bustled into the house with one arm holding groceries and the other cradling our daughter Lucia.

I play this over in my head time and again. She said: "Take one or the other for me." I went to her and tried to lift Lucia. I couldn't.

I could not lift my baby daughter. I was so weak; so riddled with arthritis and toxicity.

After Dr. Stoxen treated me and set me on my way toward wellness, I would think of that moment every time I was doing an exercise that was challenging. I would think of it every day for about a year when I more or less became a backstage hermit—working out by myself, getting strong.

Lucia was too young to notice, but around the time she learned to walk, so did I (again). And a few months later when she was totally mobile and tearing around the house, so was I, with a spring in my step. Lucia was 20 months old when she was joined by her sister, Maria Claire.

My favorite rugby league team, the Wests Tigers—they beat Russell Crowe's South Sydney Rabbitohs all the time—can take some of the credit. Well, sort of. Miki and I were cruising the streets of Leichhardt in Sydney, along with thousands of others late on the night of October 2, 2005, celebrating the Tigers' shocking victory in the National Rugby League grand final.

I guess the excitement was too much for Maria. Obviously she felt she was missing something—Tigers premiership victories are very rare—and she rushed into the world after just a couple hours of labor in the early hours of October 3.

She was a healthy 7 lbs., but gave us a scare when she emerged with the umbilical cord around her neck. Fortunately, mother and baby made a rapid recovery from the trauma. Certainly they looked healthier the next day than several of the Tigers players at the nearby Balmain Leagues Club. But that's for a different book.

My colleague Greg Page wasn't looking too good off and on during that year either. He'd lost some weight and participated in some of our cast training sessions, but was frequently sidelined by injuries. He also had been experiencing, over quite a long period, occasional fainting episodes. One of the first times he went down was in Hong Kong, just before a concert a few years earlier. It was just after SARS (Severe Acute Respiratory Syndrome) had swept through the region and we were more than a little concerned the Yellow Wiggle had contracted something serious.

But he patched himself up and stayed on the road as best he could. When he missed a tour in 2005 with illness, Sam Moran, his understudy and a regular in our cast of dancers and performers, pulled on the yellow shirt and did a great job.

By the time our beautiful boy, Antonio Carlos, arrived after a three-hour labor on April 13, 2007, I was strong enough to lift all three kids.

At 7 lbs. 7 oz., Antonio was a decent workout by himself. He had a pretty cocky look about him right from the start. I have a feeling he might be a Wests Tiger player one day, but no pressure, he can choose whatever path he desires, as long as he learns to tango at some stage.

Anthony, Miki, and the kids.

The Barefoot Family

My girls like to dress up. Princesses mainly—they have all the glittery gear and make quite a sight, especially in bare feet.

We are the barefoot family. None of us wear shoes unless we absolutely have to. We get a few strange looks, especially Miki, but she's getting used to people "tutt-tutting." After a while you tend to forget about it—and then you pop into a cafe for lunch and notice the whispering.

I admit I converted them after my sessions with Dr. Stoxen, although as Miki says, I didn't have to do too much convincing. Witnessing my turnaround was evidence enough that my new approach was working.

My wife got to experience Dr. Stoxen's expertise firsthand. Miki is a former dancer, who is again treading the boards with The Wiggles shows on occasion. However, she was struggling with extreme pain in her feet and was diagnosed by specialists in Sydney with Morton's neuroma—a build up of tissue around the nerves near the toes.

She couldn't stand up for more than about 15 minutes without the pain setting in. "And the kids were so little at the time, so it was horrible and inconvenient," she said.

Doctors said she would need surgery. Instead, Miki paid Dr. Stoxen a visit.

"I found she had a locked arch which had misaligned her gait too," he said.

He worked on her for four to five hours a day—using the methods described in this book—for three or four days, and fitted her with shoes to support her while she learned to walk properly again.

My mate, Dr. Johnny Petrozzi, using Dr. Stoxen's approach, followed up with her in Sydney over the ensuing weeks and months.

"I don't have the pain anymore. It's gone," she said.

So now we can walk everywhere in bare feet! The whole family. I also shed shoes when I work out. If I'm in a gym, I'll go for as long as they'll let me and if necessary switch to the glovelike-fitting five-finger shoes. I admit I'm more comfortable in the gym these days. People are usually pretty intrigued by my unusual routine, which I'll detail later. I only started venturing into workout spaces a little while ago, before that I used to do my routine religiously backstage before and after performances, or in my hotel room or at home. In addition to Dr. Stoxen's strengthening and supercharging routines, I slowly—very slowly—developed my own hanging exercises.

The first challenge was to change my daily schedule to make time for exercise. Paddy had gradually helped me understand it wasn't compulsory to actually work at being unhealthy on the road.

Here's what I used to do in the bad old days: On arrival at the hotel, no matter what time of day or night, I would make a bee-line for the minibar-fridge in the room. I wanted to know what chips and chocolates (despite my sensitivities) I could consume while watching whatever movie or video I could get my hands on, while lying on the comfortable hotel bed. I loved ice cream, too (despite my sensitivities).

In the morning I would go down to the lobby and eat break-fast, return to the room, lie down and, if I had time, watch a video. Then it was off to the venue where I'd nearly have a heart attack during the shows and feed my face in between performances. At the end of the day we'd roll onto the tour bus. Maybe have a snack on board between games on the X-Box and a beer or two before lying down. We'd arrive at the next city and hotel at some ridiculous hour and I'd start the same suicidal process again.

"You know you can exercise in your room?" Paddy would say. But it didn't seem possible—it certainly wasn't desirable, and I wasn't one for the gym.

I felt fat and sluggish, in addition to being virtually crippled at times with a locked spring. For the longest time, I just figured I was getting old and that was an inevitability we all faced.

However, I slowly dispensed with the world's unhealthiest daily schedule after Dr. Stoxen set me straight and showed me a

few basic hanging exercises, primarily the abdominal oblique suspension routine, to strengthen the spring around the pelvis.

The Hanging Habit

Fired by my desire to be able to pick up my daughter, I started by
taking a portable exercise bar with me everywhere, including the
venue on show day. I'd set it up somewhere where I could have a
bit of privacy and challenge myself. I started very slowly, just
hanging without feeling the entirety of my weight or simply leaning against something so as not to exert myself too much. It gave
me a chance to become familiar with *gravity*.

Instead of heading to catering after a show, I would go to my
little workout area. For weeks, about the best I could do was to lift
my feet about six inches off the ground. I was frustrated, but
remained consistent. I replaced my minibar-video routine with a
gentle exercise plan and, where possible, I would hang around on
the bar. I gradually managed to get both feet off the ground—I'd
hold it for ten seconds at a time. I couldn't do it for any longer, but
I learned to celebrate little victories like that. I did little else for
months.

I spent the better part of a year working out, mainly by myself
backstage. Eventually I braved it with a few cast members and
started using hotel gyms. I also set up a minigym on the terrace of
my home in Sydney. I bought some portable exercise rings and
incorporated them into my little routine, too. The kids just love
the rings and they seem to capture people's imaginations when I
take them to gyms.

Given a choice of rings or barbells, I know what I'd be doing.
I've gotten to the stage now where I've been told I have a
training routine that is roughly the same as a highly competitive
athlete's. Let me stress, it was my choice to go the extra few steps
with this, and I did so by inching my way forward.

If you stick with Dr. Stoxen's strengthening and supercharging routines (on a fully functioning spring) and incorporate

Dr. Gringeri's nutritional advice, complete with supplements and the occasional chiropractic adjustment, you are going to live a longer, healthier life and probably achieve fitness levels you didn't think were possible.

As I developed the discipline to exercise regularly, I enjoyed exploring unfamiliar techniques and styles. I became reasonably competent doing basic hanging over a couple of months and cultivated an interest in gymnastics and acrobatics. I bought old gymnastic instruction books and copied elementary routines, then, very slowly, challenged myself with harder exercises.

If you choose to develop a demanding routine like mine, do so cautiously. I was lucky to have the assistance and guidance of a few world-class athletes in the last few years.

What I do now, which you'll see in the next few pages, requires careful preparation and execution. Having said that, my eldest brother, Patrick, graduated to these routines recently after decades of doing little exercise. He started slowly but stuck with the program, losing nearly half his body weight in the process (he had a fair bit to lose!) and is now nearly as fit as Fatty, who has also embraced the bar and the rings.

Bikes and Bars

My days on the road have changed a little. I still stumble into hotel rooms at 3 am sometimes, but instead of hitting the mini-bar I'll eat a piece of fruit. If I'm wide awake I'll launch into a workout, using portable rings and a bar in the room.

In the morning, it's a light breakfast of fruit and one good cup of coffee and then I jump on my bike. I take a fold-up bicycle on the road and have a bit of a collection of bikes at home. If I'm in Sydney I'll ride two hours daily, at any time of the day or night. On tour, a few of the cast and crew have caught the biking bug, so we often form a little convoy riding to the venue.

That alone has been an incredible boost to my willingness to be on tour. For decades we'd pour into a bus to make the journey between hotel and venue. You'd see nothing—experience nothing—about the place you were visiting. Jumping on the bike I see what I've been missing all these years. Towns and cities I've already visited a dozen times are unveiling themselves to me for the first time. (I've got an unusual riding technique: I sit up like a rower with a straight back and pull back on the handles. It really engages the core.)

You need a good navigator, I've learned that. We rolled out of the hotel in Detroit on one recent tour and headed for the venue, only to get lost for two hours. There are some interesting neighborhoods in the Motor City, and I think I can safely say I've now seen (and survived) them all.

Our show in recent years has featured a lot of acrobatics and I've had the good fortune to include several world-class athletes in the cast, such as former Australian trampoline champion Karl Shore. We have elaborate trapeze and hanging equipment on stage as part of the show, and usually make use of it to work out prior to the performance. My bar and rings routines take about 40 minutes each. I do three to five handstands between each exercise—it helps with balance and makes me loose.

I still take my supplements and while my food sensitivities have largely subsided, I eat cautiously and healthfully between performances.

The show itself is a great workout, but I'm ready for it these days. At the end of the day, after riding back to the hotel, there is that great enveloping tiredness that comes after a day of positive physical exertion. I've never slept better.

The Routine

I developed a firm friendship with a Sydney neighbor, Dmitri Zorin, in recent years. I would do my rings routine and Dmitri would throw weights around. He would give me tips on form and the best combination of exercises, and he should know. He's a former Russian Olympic gymnastics coach and is now a member of the Australian Gymnastics Federation.

After a while, I think I helped rekindle Dmitri's enthusiasm for bar and rings. He put down the barbells and joined me. Apparently I had been fairly successful in my quest to build a comprehensive workout. Dmitri recognized many of the exercises as basic techniques—and he's since helped me take it to the next level.

Take a look at the photos of my parallel and hanging bar exercises. Don't try these if you're starting out or ill prepared. Your time will come! Even if you're an experienced gymnast do these in the presence of others so they can monitor your form. As soon it starts to slip, end the session. Three to five reps per exercise unless otherwise specified. You can opt to do three or so handstands between each exercise if you have the time and energy and feel you benefit from that stretch. Don't do handstands or inversion exercises if you're not used to them.

Tuck Front Support.

On the parallel bars start with the Tuck Front Support. Keep your arms straight and bend the knees up to your chest—get as high as you can with your knees slightly apart and hold for 20 seconds.

From that position move into Pulses. Steadily lift the knees about six inches higher, then return to the original tuck front pose. When you're up to speed do about 20 of these. They're like a reverse crunch.

Again, return to Tuck Front Support. Hold, before rotating you legs right and left in Swishes. Keep the body out front as you do 40.

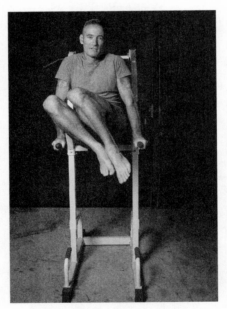

Swishes.

Proceed into L Sit. Put your legs straight out in front and don't bend your knees. Point the feet and turn your legs out from the hip. Hold that for 20 seconds.

From the L Sit go into Pike Front Support by lifting your hips up toward the ceiling. Maintain the pike position with your arms straight at all times. Go through ten reps.

The Straddle is like the L Sit but this time pull your legs apart and hold for 20 seconds.

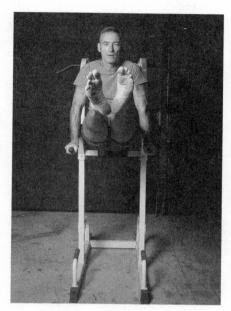

L Sit.

L Sit to Pike Front Support.

Next, the Front Support Swing: legs, arms, and body are straight—swing forward and back rhythmically, maintaining good body tension and form. Don't pike, and keep the swinging arch small at first then gradually expand it over 20 reps.

Straddle.

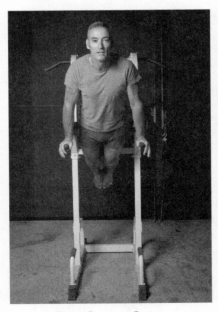

Front Support Swing.

On to the hanging bar:

Start with an L Sit. Your arms should be a full shoulder length apart. Use an overhand grip and hold for 20 seconds before moving to a Straddle and holding for 20 seconds.

L Sit.

Straddle.

Move to the L position and lift your straight legs skyward into the Upside Down L Sit and hold. Keep your back and arms straight and keep your head still.

Upside Down L Sit.

Turn and face the apparatus or the wall to move into Skin the Cat. Place your hands on the bar slightly outside the width of your shoulders. Keep the legs straight and bring your feet up. Slowly curl your legs so they are between your arms. Take care not to bump your feet against the bar. Hold, count to ten.

Next is Skin the Cat with Pulses. Pulse your legs up and down from the position ten times.

Skin the Cat with Pulses.

The Meat Hook is next. This may look difficult but it's a big test to hold your form. Start in the L sit. Bring your legs in and shift your hips and legs to each side. Do ten reps.

Meat Hook.

Turn and face the wall or apparatus. Hands grip at each
end of the bar for a Traditional Pull-Up. It's from a dead
hang—steadily haul yourself up until the chin is comfortably over the bar. Don't swing your body as you do ten
reps, use only upper body strength.

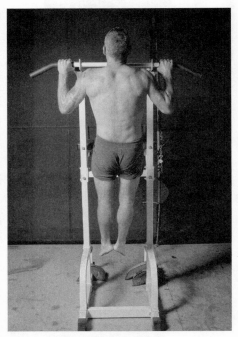

Traditional Pull-Up.

Follow it with ten Tuck Pull-Ups: from a tuck position, rotate
the torso so you are horizontal.

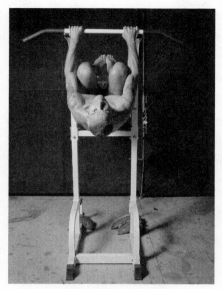

Tuck Pull-Up.

Upside-Down?

I do some inverting on the apparatus in my extended routine, but my *upside-down* time is, for the most part, handstands. There are many proponents of inversion therapy who believe there is extensive therapeutic value in the practice; however, there's also considerable medical concern about some potential dangers.

Supporters believe inversion relieves pressure on discs and nerve roots, can help strengthen ligaments, and improves posture and flexibility.

But as Dr. Stoxen noted, many in the scientific community believe it's possible to get many of the same benefits by simply lying down.

Certainly people with heart disease, high blood pressure, eye diseases, or those who are pregnant shouldn't be considering an inversion workout. Changes in the way the heart pumps blood and the way we breathe when inverted put some at risk.

Even if you're healthy and not pregnant, it's a good idea to consult a doctor before employing even the easiest inversion techniques. If and when you initiate a program, have someone with you in case assistance is required to get out of the apparatus, or if health problems arise.

Anthony was 45 when he learned to do splits.

The kids love the rings.

9

Why We Do It

We've been lucky with our cast, our turnover is pretty minimal—we've always had great loyalty from, and talent among, the performers.

We didn't really cart around a big troupe until the late 1990s, and initially we employed a lot of kids from our then choreographer's dance studio. But as the show evolved and we started hitting bigger stages we got a great bunch of young adults in. Traveling the world with a dozen or so ambitious and talented performers has a few special challenges. Certainly we wanted them to abide by the same *rules* as us.

Occasional boozy dinners, parties, even romances happen on the road. We're better matchmakers than those online dating services—marriages have resulted: Lyn and Sam, Paddy and Charmaine, but for the most part touring is just a lot of hard work. For a group playing three concerts a day starting at 10 am, staying up until 10 pm to watch a movie is a wild night.

I'm afraid you won't catch Dorothy flinging TV sets into the hotel pool or Wags propping up the bar every night until closing. And Jeff doesn't fall inebriated and unconscious into the hotel garden. He may be the sleepy one, but remember, he doesn't drink. However, many years ago in Adelaide, the young performer who was doing duty daily in the bulky Henry the Octopus getup was celebrating her birthday. We had a great party, but consumed a bit too much alcohol.

The next day, the drive out to the venue for the shows was a little "tragic." Worst for wear was the birthday girl. The poor young woman looked and felt abominable, but the show "must go on" and, like a prisoner donning an execution hood, she slowly and fearfully placed Henry's heavy head over her ash-gray face. Henry's role was largely restricted to doing the occasional dance in those days. I would hold on to one of the octopus arms/legs and do a few accompanying steps.

OK. I couldn't resist. I suggested loudly: "Henry, why don't you spin around to the music?" Whirl completed, Henry was about to make haste for backstage.

"That was great, Henry," I said. "How about we do it again—wheeeeee . . .

"And again . . . and again . . . one more time!"

No one in the audience suspected anything untoward as Henry suddenly scampered offstage in the direction of the nearest bathroom.

Unfortunately, the octopus head isn't the easiest thing to remove. Suffice to say, it had to be "put down" sometime later after several attempts to clean and purify it were resoundingly unsuccessful.

We don't rule with an iron fist but there is the obvious stuff—get to the show on time, don't mess up your routine too often, don't commit a terrorist act, and don't dance on tables (unless you're a *very* good dancer).

We do stress a few things: we expect everybody associated with us to nurture a positive relationship with the audience on and offstage and it's important that the performers respect the work they're doing, however different it might be from what they're used to. We try and ensure that this runs all the way through the organization, including our touring character productions such as *The Dorothy the Dinosaur Show* or *The Captain Feathersword Show*, which play dates in Australia, the U.K., and the U.S. These productions feature our Wiggles costume characters along with an emcee and a few dancers. They are a great way for us to have a presence in areas we might not be able to get to with the main show, or to keep things bubbling along between visits.

Dorothy, along with Captain Feathersword, is our most popular character. We've always tried to make her gentle enough to not be in any way threatening (a big green and yellow dinosaur can appear intimidating) but robust enough to take on any challenge. Our former choreographer Leeanne "Ashes" Ashley kind of wrote the blueprint for Dorothy. She was the first full-time dinosaur and knew the potential to actually point to someone's characteristics by moving in a particular way.

"I liked her being kind of girly and innocent but she was boisterous," she said. "I'd run like a girl with my arms, but not my legs. She wasn't to be too sweet." Ashes stepped out of the costume in later years to coordinate our attempts to be passable dancers.

I wonder what Dr. Stoxen would make of Dorothy's gait.

While the character costumes can be cumbersome, they can serve a useful purpose offstage from time to time. On one trip we didn't have much room for props and personal baggage after we managed to get the costumes into the luggage area of a small plane that was transporting us to the remote town of Windorah in southwest Queensland. This was an area where the temperatures can soar to 110° F in the day but plummet to the freezing point on a clear night.

Everyone packed a bare minimum for the trip because we only had two small planes for cast, crew, and gear and it was fairly cramped at the Windorah Hotel, too—we were all slotted into just two rooms.

Unfortunately, I failed to pack enough clothes to counter the frigid night air. Sleeping on the floor in one of the rooms, I looked around for whatever I could find to keep him warm. One of the crew was a new guy who had no doubt expected something unusual on tour with The Wiggles, but nothing prepared him for waking up in the morning next to Wags the Dog. At least it kept me warm.

It's extremely important that the productions feature performances on a par with the main show and we often interchange cast. My niece Clare, who has regularly been on the road with The Wiggles, is the current dance captain, and her brother Luke is tour manager.

They have the tall task of making sure high standards are maintained and for the most part that's achievable given the quality talent we've had at our disposal over the years.

We get a lot of really extraordinary people auditioning. Clearly a few of them see the gigs as stepping stones to greater things, which is fine, but sometimes we have to remind them they first have a job to do—a highly defined role to play—with us.

I remember a few years back when an upcoming actor was playing the role of Captain Feathersword in one of the character shows. My brother Paul and our then choreographer Leeanne turned up to see how the new charge was progressing. It quickly became clear he had a wonderful voice, but his performance was uneven.

Of course Paddy Paddick, THE Captain Feathersword, has created a very specific character. Emulating that character is the actor's role. But this young thespian seemed to ignore what had been asked of him, preferring to create some strange hybrid of Captain Hook and a private school master. Furthermore he was ignoring some basic Wiggle rules such as never referring to the audience as "boys and girls." Not only is it potentially condescending, it depersonalizes our interaction with concert-goers. We either call children by their names or use terms like "everyone" when we address an audience—it's called, rather coldly, creating an "illusion of intimacy." Bottom line is, the *finger wagging* approach of some entertainers has no place under The Wiggles banner.

Paul and Ashes quietly pulled the cast aside for "notes," a common practice in the theater allowing those in charge of a production to pass on their impressions to the cast. Unfortunately, the would-be Feathersword was having none of it.

"I need a day's notice to take notes," he insisted to Ashes and Paul, two of the least pompous people on the planet. The temperature suddenly soared in the room and other cast members fled like citizens anticipating a gun battle in a Wild West saloon.

My brother was going to give the actor notes "a day early" whether he liked it or not: "Now, listen just for a minute," he began.

"Don't you point your finger at me," the actor barked indignantly. "I was in *Cats!*"

And with that, The Wiggles waved good-bye and wished him good luck on Broadway.

Man Down

Frighteningly pale and as inanimate as a rock, Pagey lies on the floor in a room backstage. On the other side of a stage curtain, the 5,000-strong audience bubbles over with preconcert excitement. They sing along to the recorded overture:

"Hot potato, hot potato . . ."

Minutes from the scheduled start of the show, the crew scramble: The worried cast tries to make sense of what's going on.

"Potato, potato, potato, potato, potato . . ."

Pagey, not for the first time, has fainted without warning—surely a sign that more than 15 years of touring and recording is holding him accountable.

"Cold spaghetti, cold spaghetti . . ."

Sam squeezes into one of Pagey's yellow shirts. We make quick adjustments to the show—a song is dropped, a bit of choreography is changed, and we all understand we need to pick up a few of Greg's lines.

"Mash banana, mashed banana . . ."

The nine members of the dance troupe line up at stage left—word has filtered through that Pagey, who has been walking with the assistance of a stick sometimes lately, has fainted again.

"Woo!"

Showtime.

I bellow: "Chookers!" our version of the theatrical good luck call of "break a leg." Smiles switch on, heads lift high, and we bounce onto the stage and try and give children 90 minutes of uncomplicated musical joy.

Pagey, meanwhile, was tended to by staff with medical qualifications. He faced another potentially frustrating battery of medical tests. Over about seven years, Greg was occasionally breathless for no apparent reason, or would feel dizzy when he bent down to be at eye level with children.

He thought it was asthma. It wasn't. He thought it was exhaustion, it wasn't.

Gradually, the occasional episodes became frequent. He was tired all the time and could do little else than lie down before and after shows. Sometimes he would bump into walls. He had to head home early from a U.S. tour in 2006 because he simply wasn't up to it.

There were months of hand-wringing concern from family, friends, and colleagues. Eventually Pagey was diagnosed with orthostatic intolerance, a condition under the broad umbrella of dysautonomia—a chronic disorder of the autonomic nervous system (yep, the nervous system that controls all the other bodily functions). Basically blood isn't efficiently distributed through the body, leading to a range of symptoms including fainting, difficulty with speech, and extreme fatigue.

While not life-threatening, the condition made it impossible for Pagey to continue performing with anything like the regularity and intensity we require in The Wiggles. He knew it, we knew it. He needed to step away to be able to concentrate on getting well.

It was wrenching. We'd kind of grown up together, doing this thing as a tight unit for so long, even though the memory of a children's entertainment booker in Sydney turning us down when we started out in 1991 was still fresh. So on November 30, 2006, we announced Greg Page would stop touring and recording to concentrate on managing his health. He made a farewell video in which he handed over the yellow shirt to Sam.

The poor bloke was so sick, even making the video was a chore. He could only manage a couple of lines at a time. It looked like he'd have trouble finishing it at one stage.

Of course there was understandable widespread speculation—from the front page of the *New York Times* to the *Telegraph* in Sydney and perhaps more importantly, the notes we received from our young audience—whether The Wiggles would be able to continue to flourish without our talented lead singer.

Stepping away from the spotlight was a personal tragedy for Greg and his family, and could have brought everyone associated with The Wiggles to their knees. Obviously we all considered the merits of continuing a creative and business process that had grown organically with Pagey as an integral part, but to bring the curtain down on The Wiggles would have been counter to the spirit and intent we had worked tirelessly to maintain from the start.

The foundations of the enterprise were as steady as ever. Sam has an exceptional voice and was already armed with firsthand knowledge of what it means to "be a Wiggle."

We hit the road.

Sam Moran took over the yellow shirt.

The Wiggles enjoying London.

The Wiggles love Whoopi Goldberg.

Hanging with Kylie Minogue.

Onward

Even before Pagey stepped away, we had been making quiet inroads in the U.K. While there was still the odd British entertainment executive anxious to tell us how "cheesy" we were, we established great working relationships with a number of people and companies. For the last six years or so, we've toured the U.K. and Ireland regularly and enjoyed playing to full houses in some great venues there—sure beats the holiday camps we were restricted to on some of those early visits.

We continue to tour Asia—Hong Kong, Singapore, Taipei, Beijing, and Shanghai—and we get to see our friends in the U.S., New Zealand, and Canada regularly. We also have a TV presence in South America and the Middle East (where my sister Anne lives with her beautiful family) and we've managed to play in Dubai and the Malaysian capital, Kuala Lumpur.

For a considerable time, we backed ventures effectively cloning The Wiggles in Taiwan and set up a Spanish-language version of the group. We enjoyed success with some of the *local* Wiggles, but eventually found there was a big demand to see the *real* Wiggles in concerts and on television. In Japan, for example, they dub us from Monday to Friday but run the original production on Saturdays (such is the importance of learning English as a second language).

A big challenge is finding the time between preexisting obligations to get to places we'd love to visit. High on the list currently is Argentina, where we're thrilled to have a growing audience. Carlos Gardel territory: El Zorzal Criollo!

Over the years we've dipped our feet into different business ventures, including theme park rides and play centers, and we started developing a few non-Wiggles concepts like *The Kingdom of Paramithi*, a fairy-tale television series, and *Baby Antonio's Circus*, featuring a couple of my favorite things—my youngest born and acrobatics. It's all hugely challenging, but to be honest, my main passion is and always will be the show and the sound and look of our DVDs.

Despite the best efforts of my brother Paul and our business manager Mike Conway to bring an element of conventional business planning to our process, we still try and focus first and foremost on what instinctively feels right.

If we made decisions by committee we wouldn't have been a band in the first place. When we first came to America there was a little bit of talk about our apparent "lack of diversity." Three Caucasian Australians and an Asian-Australian: What about people of color, and where were the women?

We fully understood the need to reflect the diversity in the communities we were part of and seeking to entertain, but our venture developed organically. We weren't put together in some Hollywood studio executive's office. We probably would have been better off with a woman in the group to some extent—even if only from a musical standpoint—but the fact was, I was just too shy to have much to do with women when the band tumbled together at college. The only musicians on my radar at the time were the two tall guys at college, my mate Jeff, my brothers, and the rest of The Cockroaches.

All I was thinking at the time was how I could make good music for children that reflected their interests and celebrated their desire to sing and dance. It was a pleasant change to be playing with a few different people in The Wiggles, but for years we still drew on our immediate circle of family and friends. Tony Henry, our Cockroaches drummer (yes, Henry the Octopus is named after Henners), was a regular in the studio, and my brothers and cousins played roles. Also, when we cobbled together our cheap little videos we didn't go through central casting for the extras and the dancers, we drew on our families mainly because we didn't have any money and that family vibe was what we were all about, anyway.

Over the years we incorporated more diversity among the talent we utilized on stage and screen, and we certainly ensured there was more of a gender and ethnicity mix in some of the off-shoot productions. But I'm afraid I'm a fourth-generation Australian with Irish, French, Italian, and English heritage who married a beautiful Greek Australian, and that's that.

Keeping tabs on everything becomes tough at times. Certainly there was a period in the late 1990s when we felt we were relying too heavily on accountants and lawyers (and were paying a pretty penny to do so). But having Paul and Mike since then has taken a bit of the pressure off.

Muz, in particular, no longer has to review every merchandising proposal—although we do sign off on things. We try to ensure everything under our banner is generally useful.

Toys and playtime facilitators are generally considered essential in the development of a child's motor and language skills. At their best, they serve to aid the child's storytelling process—a central component in healthy development. But we also understand that parents don't want to be swamped by advertising and pressure selling.

We know there's a fine line between maintaining and promoting early childhood values and operating in the commercial arena, and that's why we've always proceeded cautiously. As Muz said: "Sometimes we make mistakes, but hopefully we stick to what's developmentally appropriate most of the time."

Similarly, being on TV necessitates paying careful attention to the specifics of the content produced and the broader issue of children as viewers. Our goal is to entertain, but every form of communication carries messages, so we try and work within the boundaries of fundamentally sound values and the concepts that are part of every toddler's world. There's no hidden irony with The Wiggles and we're not out to bang a drum about adult *issues*—because neither is your child.

We're not as didactic as some, but we know what we are trying to do onstage and on the screen.

Over the years, there's been a continuous debate about how much time children should or should not spend in front of the television or playing with other media. In many quarters, selective exposure to appropriate television content by preschoolers is believed to help promote language skills and prosocial behavior—concepts concertedly promoted by The Wiggles in performance.

The bottom line from our perspective is that we all should set limits and make sure, for example, television isn't a replacement for adequate physical activity. There should be a balance between television and reading, and interesting programs should be followed up with books.

Little People, Huge Hearts

It's great when we hear about parents and caregivers watching our shows with their children, participating in the music, and talking the kids through subjects as they arise.

We've been thrilled on a number of occasions over the years to talk to parents whose children have enjoyed positive experiences—sometimes life-changing—when watching the show or a DVD.

We wouldn't, for a minute, claim to be much more than entertainers who are trying to be responsible. But it's both rewarding and startling, in a sense, to know that sometimes we make a connection with the little ones that genuinely helps them.

Maryanne, an Australian mom, was as much amused as anything else at her boy Phoenix's obsession with The Wiggles.

Phoenix was a bit of magic. Maryanne and her husband had all but given up on their hope to have children, but after selling off all of their major possessions (house, car, etc.) and preparing to ship out of Australia for a life in the U.S., their little boy arrived on the scene.

"We'd quit jobs and given everything away to the Salvation Army, so we were stuck in an empty unit in Melbourne with nothing," she said. But her husband, Chris, secured a position, and soon life took on the ebullient though occasionally exhausting rhythm dictated by the presence of an active kid in a small space.

Phoenix was a timid boy but generally in robust health, so Maryanne and Chris were worried and surprised when he became ill enough to warrant a hospital visit. Worry soon became panic as 22-month-old Phoenix's condition nose-dived. "Terror, sheer terror," Maryanne recalled her reaction.

Over four days, a round-the-clock battle to arrest the boy's deterioration couldn't prevent his slumping into a critical state. All doctors could say was he had some sort of virus. Ghostly white, enduring a fever of obscene proportions, and wiped out by dehydration, Phoenix's weak cries of "Mommy" gradually faded.

"They told us to say good-bye in the emergency room," Maryanne said.

The unthinkable was happening. And it was only a matter of time . . .

Desperate to try and ensure his last moments might be in some way uplifting, Maryanne got a Wiggles video from the nurses on duty and asked them to slot it into the machine. Within minutes of Wake Up Jeff starting to play, Phoenix opened his eyes and tried to focus. Staff played The Wiggles nonstop. After about three hours, Phoenix was concentrating on the video and calling for his mother. He was discharged seven hours later—doctors no wiser about his illness, Maryanne said, but convinced he had bounced back after teetering on the brink of death.

Let me assure you, I'm not saying The Wiggles are a cure for mysterious life-threatening conditions, but I dip into the mailbag sometimes and am utterly overwhelmed at the impact you can have by trying to play a small but positive role in kids' lives.

Sometimes too, we get the most extraordinary news when we're on the road. You know you need to do *something*, but what?

Back in 2003 we got word of the awful story of a toddler, Sophie Delezio, being one of two victims in an incident involving a burning car that crashed into her preschool. She had third degree burns to 85 percent of her body and would eventually lose both her legs.

On hearing she was a Wiggles fan, we wanted to get something to her. So my sister-in-law Pauline arranged to drop off a care package of merchandise at the hospital. Unexpectedly Pauline ended up being invited by Sophie's mom to say hello to her brave girl. Sophie, Pauline discovered, had Wiggles-brand Band-Aids all over her little body. Turned out she used them to tell the doctors where the pain was.

Her mom also revealed that Sophie's unthinkable trauma of being trapped under a burning car was so immense, doctors had advised against discussing the event with her. But apparently one of her favorite DVDs was a Wiggles video featuring New York firefighters describing the fire-retardant material they wear: "I should have had that," she said, unprompted, opening the door to a potential treatment of intolerable psychological hurt.

We don't construe these occurrences as notches in our belts or proof of our worth or otherwise, but we do celebrate them, it would be wrong not to. We also marvel at something as basic as kids emulating my loudly professed taste for fruit salad—as noted in one of our songs. Or maybe it is children showing a sudden, overdue interest in learning colors, shapes, and numbers.

In the case of Savannah Stalnaker it was cuddling. A brain cancer survivor, Savannah came to the Stalnakers in West Virginia as a foster child, not speaking, and clearly "mad at the world."

"She had a bonding disorder," Cindy Stalnaker said. "She was angry . . . she scratched herself, it was very difficult."

Savannah, however, quickly formed an attachment to The Wiggles, which presented Cindy with an opportunity. Attending her first ever Wiggles concert, Savannah was enthralled, "alive like never before," and afterward she rewarded Cindy with more than she had hoped for. "She gave me an unprompted hug. Our first." Savannah still faces enormous challenges. She is engaged in a struggle to merely survive, although the ferocity of her attachment disorder is waning.

A hug—you can never overestimate the value of a hug.

Hope

My dad wooed my mother, in part, by reciting Shakespearean sonnets to her and failing to disclose he wasn't the author. It was an extension of his little business as a teenager at boarding school where he'd charge some of the less articulate country boys a few "bob" to write letters to attract the attention of girls who otherwise wouldn't look at them sideways.

He was mischievous and wonderful. He gave everyone he met, even the worst druggies and drunks, real hope.

Over the last 20 years, I've been surrounded by the personification of that notion—millions of preschool-age kids with every magnificent possibility in front of them. Along with my father and family they were my salvation more than once.

But I was scraping along the bottom there for some considerable time on this journey. I not only lost my way a few times, I had all but given up on the idea of seeing myself as being deserving of making the trip. Illness and injury were a product of my physical deterioration but equally a reflection of the collapse of my spirit.

I needed the help of some very innovative people to get out of that deep dark space, but my escape only came after I took responsibility to try and claw my way back into the light, rather than waiting around for something to lift me—the professional miracle workers of the medical profession, their pills, and medications.

I've always said I prefer to get on with things; not to wait around for perfection, because when you do nothing gets done. Yet there I was, for decades, waiting to be rescued; thankful when an attempt was made, but inevitably disappointed when a miracle failed to eventuate.

The United States, the United Kingdom, and Australia are among the world's wealthiest countries and, we're continually told, have the globe's most advanced medical technology, which would be great if we weren't all so sick. That's because, largely inadvertently, we have bought a bill of goods that's been disguised as hope.

I'm not denigrating genuine scientific and medical advances, but where is the logic of taking medications and undergoing sometimes devastating procedures in order to try and stabilize conditions that have been brought on by other medications and misguided treatments?

When we started out, we were sometimes criticized, even abused, for being four men talking in simple terms to children. But here's what we have learned, in no uncertain terms: Simplicity, as Leonardo Da Vinci said, is the ultimate sophistication.

Common sense is extraordinarily insightful. Employ it when you consider your health and fitness situation, allow it to investigate the credibility of the two approaches to wellness we've talked about in this book.

The Big Show

I still mutter to Miki from time to time about how disconsolate I get on the road and occasionally think maybe it's time to take a step back.

"But then, when you're home you can't sit still for five seconds," she said recently. "You love it; you live it twenty-four hours a day. There's still plenty of work to be done."

True, the mission to entertain hasn't changed—making the ordinary, extraordinary and trying to gently coax children to head in the direction of developmental milestones. If nothing else we've always wanted to be a safe haven for kids, facilitators of healthy personal exploration and self-awareness.

The novelty for parents of watching four young men singing and dancing with their kids might have changed a little, but perhaps there is added value in seeing old guys like Fatty and me doing stuff athletically that might be unexpected.

We've rejuvenated our stage show and tinkered with our production and touring schedules from time to time in recent years to accommodate our families. Some relationships with longtime international partners have changed and we had to realign the ownership structure of our venture when Pagey departed. That was a longer process than we expected, but as a former shareholder he was very well looked after.

Twenty years of between 300 to 500 shows annually has provided an unfair share of joyful moments, invaluable insight into our kids, professional satisfaction, and indirectly, a personal rescue mission.

It's been satisfying to receive some formal acknowledgment from universities and our own government in recent years that we've been of some use to the early childhood education sector and made a mark in entertainment, but I know what I've received in return and that knowledge is humbling.

There will be more shows, fun, achievements and, no doubt, occasional heartbreak in the future, but for the moment, let's bring this to a close. If you've been to a Wiggles performance, you'll know the drill. For the final big number, let's all stand up—out of your seats, mothers, fathers, grandparents, caregivers, and children—and join in.

Let's dance together, smile unreservedly, and hug our kids. Let's all be wide-eyed about the world for a few more minutes. Then, when the last note is played, streamers will fall from above to cover us in color.

Lift our children up. Lift them high . . . till next time.

Frequently Asked Questions

For Dr. Stoxen: The Human
Spring Doctor

How can you tell the spring in the arch of the foot is likely locked?
Usually there will be pain and tightness, but sometimes we've grown so accustomed to our feet being *tender* we overlook how imperative it is to correct the issue. To confirm a locked spring use the self-examination techniques in the book: the arch wiggle test, the toe lift, and look at how you walk.

How long does it take to release the spring?
I perform at least 10 passes through the pattern of muscle spasms that bind the spring. It can take up to 35 hours of work in the most severe cases. These patients are either chronic cases or facing back surgery for herniated discs or worse.

   If you suspect you are a severe case, take this book to a professional and have them help you by employing the techniques outlined as a guide.

Once released, for how long will it remain "unlocked"?
If your human spring is completely released and you have strengthened and supercharged the spring (and wear supportive footwear when you know the suspension muscles will become fatigued) it will last a lifetime.

Do flat feet contribute to the locking of arch springs?

All feet are engineered differently, though all feet have a spring mechanism. It's not important if you have a flat foot or a high arch. What matters is that your spring is released and the spring suspension system muscles are strong enough to handle the activity you wish to do.

Barefoot runners have noted an increase in the arch height over time. Bones will change their position when muscles increase in strength. We see this with other areas of the body like in the curves of the spine as well as in the chest, back, and shoulders.

How long does it take to do a useful spring strengthening session?

The spring strengthening can take minutes to more than an hour depending on how fast you move through the training. You should always do the spring release before the spring strengthening sessions. That takes at least 15 minutes and up to an hour if you have areas to release before starting the strengthening routine.

Spring strengthening is mostly a lower-body exercise program. It should be done on the same days as your lower-body routine. I recommend you do it at least twice but no more than three times a week.

How can you tell if you've been successful unlocking the spring mechanism?

Move methodically through the self-examination and self-test sections. If you have a healthy spring you'll be able to *pass* all the tests. There won't be any lingering spasms as outlined in the release section. If you have pain doing any of the impact activities you need to check again.

How many people have locked springs?

Tens of millions. Think about how many people wear shoes every day of their lives. If they wear them for long enough they will endure a locked spring. It is estimated that 70 million people suffer from chronic pain in America. All have a locked spring.

Do children's springs ever lock? If so, should they follow the same guidelines?

Yes, increasingly so as more children wear shoes than in previous decades. More are overweight and overloading the human spring.

The lack of barefoot free play (moving in multiple directions) on a regular basis means their human spring mechanism is locking up sooner in life. The guidelines are the same for kids and adults.

Shoes are compulsory in many gyms. Is there a compromise between bare feet and shod?

If you are training your feet with the spring strengthening you cannot wear shoes. If you must, look for minimalist shoes to train in. There are many different styles. The key is finding a foot covering that inhibits natural motion the least.

What do you think about those shape and tone as you walk shoes?

Shoe companies claim that these work the leg muscles more, thus burning more calories and shaping your frame. These shoes actually force you into a new way of walking. Your brain memorizes that. If you wear them enough the memory pattern of the natural way to walk is replaced by the new shape-up shoe way.

There is only one healthy way to walk and that is barefoot with the pattern recommended in the book. Wearing a binding device on your foot and training the body in movements that are counter to the way the body is engineered is detrimental to your health.

If I have fibromyalgia or chronic fatigue how long does it take for those conditions to be affected by a spring release and exercise program?

The fact that you are diagnosed with a chronic condition like fibromyalgia or chronic fatigue means you have had a locked spring mechanism for years and it is severe. The amount of time it takes each person to rebound from that has to do with many factors such as height and weight, BMI (Body Mass Index), how locked the spring is, how long it has been locked, overall health, and how bad the gait is.

A reminder: If your foot rolls out of the safe range between supination and pronation you must wear footwear to maintain the foot in the safe range until you can develop the spring suspension system muscles to do it for you. If you don't you will never heal and your conditions won't improve.

Can you play sports with a locked spring?
You can play sports with a locked spring but you won't be as quick, balanced, or agile if your mechanism is locked.

You won't have as much free spring energy so you will tire faster, affecting stamina, which is especially detrimental to long-distance sports.

You will be at particularly high risk for sudden acute injuries like sprains, strains, tears, and herniations, as well as chronic overuse conditions discussed in this book.

Is swimming good for the human spring? What about other activities?
Swimming is a non-weight-bearing activity. The spring works with impact in the weight-bearing joints. Swimming does not specifically build spring suspension system strength.

Can old people benefit from any of these techniques?
Everyone can benefit from this approach. Each person should evaluate the integrity of their human spring based on the tests provided. The strengthening and supercharging should be based on the integrity of the spring strength rather than age. I have patients in their 30s with severely weak spring suspension systems who couldn't walk without severe pain. It took two to three weeks of aggressive work to release their spring and allow them to walk pain free. I also have an 89-year-old patient

who could not walk after a back injury but after just a few treatments he was able to walk a mile and run several blocks easily. He now releases his human spring every day before training and is able to work out like a 20-year-old with no pain anywhere in his body.

Is it painful to try and unlock the spring? If it hurts, does it necessarily mean damage is being done?

When you work on the muscle spasms that restrict or lock the human spring there is some pain during the deep-tissue work. It is not causing damage, merely hurting when the treatment is applied on the inflamed, tonically contracted muscles. Pain is a gauge that you should use to determine the health of your human spring. Do not think of it as a bad thing when you are doing the treatment.

For Dr. Gringeri: The Human Engine Doctor

Who can benefit most from the human engine approach?

Anyone who would prefer to improve body function rather than treat illness or disease with medications. At the very least it helps those wanting to exert some control over their condition, by providing knowledge and the understanding it's not necessary to blindly accept all traditional medical approaches and prescriptions.

Is chiropractic treatment safe for children?

Not only is it safe, it is vital to the health of children. I gently manipulate newborns. The birth process is often ravaging to a child's neck and fragile nerves. Chiropractic has been shown to be unsurpassed in the treatment of colic and is often effective in relieving the pain of ear infections.

Toddlers who fall a few hundred times while learning to walk do well to get the spine realigned. Properly applied, this approach can help children reach their optimal potential. Where medicine only treats disease, the human engine approach is designed to help us to reach our potential.

What about aging adults with brittle bones?

There are a number of techniques in chiropractic employing extremely low force that are very safe even for older patients with brittle bones. It's vital for the elderly that we optimize the nervous system, improving respiratory and digestive system function.

What's in this approach for people who are healthy and already eat well?

For most adults, the most neglected part of their health is their spine. Having your spine evaluated and treated can improve your nervous system function and therefore your overall health. Even if you don't have any obvious symptoms, having the digestive system evaluated and finding a suitable program of improved nutrition and digestion is of obvious benefit.

Most of us have eaten more than our share of cooked foods and likely indulged in low-quality fast foods, and that's reason enough to take action.

We get used to our life and think we are fine. We just don't always know how much better it can be.

Are you suggesting diabetics throw away their medication?

Not at all! I always tell my patients that my job is to help you get healthier and get your body working better. As your health improves, often your blood glucose normalizes. As it does, the decision to continue, reduce, or eliminate your medication is between you and your medical doctor.

Why is a chiropractor talking about diabetes?

Chiropractic is the largest nondrug health care system in the U.S. We help the patient implement the very programs their doctors want them to do—often better exercise and eating routines.

Is the treatment for people suffering from Parkinson's in any way intrusive?

Not in the least. Parkinson's patients have so much trouble moving and controlling their bodies, they usually welcome anything that calms them down and helps them improve the movement control. These patients get specific help with digestion, which is a big issue for them. The formulations we provide improve their digestion and common constipation issues and they see an increase in energy, controlled motion, and balance.

It's not like we're in the third world, we have the most advanced medical technology available to us, why do we need alternative approaches?

If you ask 100 people if nutrition improves their health, they will almost all say yes. And yet nutrition is called alternative health care. Also, the laying of hands and spinal manipulation has been around for over 5,000 years.

Most medicated people recognize the drugs they take are toxic—using toxic substances to restore health should be considered alternative.

Out of the 37 industrialized nations the World Health Organization has ranked, the U.S. ranks last in health and wellness. Americans also spend more per person on drugs than anyone else in the world. An alternative to this situation is overdue.

If it's so effective why aren't all doctors doing what you do?

Doctor means "teacher." MDs are trained in disease, diagnosis, pathology, and identifying symptoms to treat with their medicines. They are teachers of medicine. The medical schools don't teach much nutrition, function, or wellness, although with many of us going green, I believe that they will be soon.

We want safe, nontoxic health care and the medical profession will come to understand this, although traditions and dogmas don't change overnight.

Should we completely give up cooked food?

No. Continue to love your steak and salad but also try eating more raw foods and drink lots of green smoothies. You'll notice an increase in energy levels.

Many natural health care practitioners use a totally raw food diet to help the body heal from some of the most serious illnesses. Eating a good percentage (maybe 50 percent) of your foods, especially fruits and vegetables, raw is a great start. It will take the burden off of your digestive system and will provide your body with enzymes and much-needed fiber to keep you healthy.

You say environmental factors are influencing our health. What's the biggest threat?

It is unclear what the biggest threat is. A lot of research on diabetes points to toxic exposure: antibiotics and other medications, chemicals in plastics, arsenic in our drinking water, and even excessive air pollution. If toxicity (poisoning) is the cause of diabetes, then in the next 39 years one out of three people will be poisoned to the point that they will have a serious illness. Parkinson's disease has also been heavily linked to toxic exposure. If we want a truly healthy environment in which to live, we need more organic foods, less chemicals in the home, and more research dollars on nontoxic health treatment.

Do you consult with traditional medical doctors?

I am very open to working with medical doctors. I practiced with a medical doctor for more than five years and have referred many of my patients to MDs. I sometimes form health teams with MDs in the interest of patients.

Glossary

These have been compiled in consultation with Drs. Stoxen and Gringeri in the context of their relevance and use in their respective approaches.

Aerobic   Exercise geared to provide a sufficient cardiovascular overload to stimulate increases in cardiac output.

Adjustment   Application of force to a vertebral articulation to restore biomechanical and neurological function.

Asthma   A chronic inflammatory disease of the airways.

Biomechanics   The field of study using the laws of physics and engineering to describe motion of body segments, and the forces that act upon them during activity.

Carbohydrates   An abundant organic compound. Ingested carbohydrates are sugars and starches, which are metabolized into glucose, or assembled into glycogen and stored in the liver and muscle for future use.

Chiropractic   From the Greek words meaning done by hand. Grounded in the principle that the body can heal itself when the skeletal system is correctly aligned and the nervous system is functioning properly.

Chronic   Persisting for a long time.

Circulatory system   Consisting of the heart, blood vessels, and lymphatics. The system that circulates blood and lymph throughout the body.

Diabetes   Any disorder characterized by excessive urine excretion. When used alone, the term refers to diabetes mellitus.

Diabetes mellitus   A broadly applied term used to denote a complex group of syndromes that have in common a disturbance in the oxidation and utilization of glucose, which is secondary to a malfunction of the beta cells of the pancreas, whose function is the production and release of insulin. Because insulin is involved in the metabolism of carbohydrates, proteins, and fats, diabetes is not limited to a disturbance of glucose homeostasis alone.

Digestion   The conversion of food into chemical substances that can be absorbed and assimilated.

Digestive leukocytosis   A rise in the number of leukocytes—white blood cells—after eating (usually after eating cooked foods).

Digestive system   The organs, structures, and accessory glands of the digestive tube of the body through which food passes from the mouth to the esophagus, stomach, and intestines. The accessory glands secrete the digestive enzymes, which break down food substances in preparation for absorption into the bloodstream.

Dorsi flexion   Movement that brings the top of the foot toward the lower leg.

Elastic deformity   When the spring deforms, stores energy, then re-forms to its original shape and in doing so releases the energy.

Endocrine system (hormones)   Consists of the endocrine glands and the hormones they secrete.

Enzymes   Proteins produced by living organisms and functioning as biochemical catalysts.

Engine   A machine that converts energy into mechanical force or motion.

External force   Force exerted on the body from the outside. For example: a backpack.

Fats Substances composed of liquids or fatty acids and occurring in various forms or consistencies ranging from oil to tallow.

Fibromyalgia Muscle and connective tissue pain.

Foot abduction When the foot rotates laterally (wave out).

Foot adduction When the foot rotates medially (wave in).

Foot eversion Outward rotation (a sideways movement) of the foot so that the sole faces laterally (scoop out).

Foot inversion Inward rotation (a sideways movement) of the foot so that the sole faces medially (scoop in).

Forefoot The area in the front (fore) of the foot, including the five metatarsals and the fourteen phalange bones and surrounding soft tissues.

Fuel Something consumed to produce energy.

Gait The manner or style of walking.

Hind foot The posterior third of the foot consisting of the talus, the calcaneus, and the accompanying joints.

Hip abduction The thigh moves away from the center of the body.

Hip adduction The thigh moves toward the center of the body.

Hip extension Hip straightening.

Hip flexion Forward bending where the thigh(s) come closer to the torso.

Hip lateral rotation The thigh rotates away from the center of body.

Hip medial rotation The thigh rotates toward the center of body.

Hooke's Law In mechanics and physics, the extension or compression of a spring is in direct proportion to the load applied to it.

Human spring The combined spring mechanisms of the seven floors of the human body.

Immune   The reaction of an organism's body to foreign materials, including the production of antibodies.

Inflammation   A protective tissue response to injury or destruction of tissues, which serves to destroy, dilute, or wall off both the injurious agent and the injured tissues. The signs of acute inflammation are pain, heat, redness, swelling, and loss of function.

Insert   A removable insole worn for a number of purposes, including daily wear comfort, foot and joint pain relief from arthritis, orthopedic correction, smell reduction, and athletic performance.

Insulin   A hormone produced by the pancreas that regulates blood glucose levels by stimulating the absorption of sugars into the cells.

Internal force   Force exerted on the body from the inside. For example: muscle spasms compressing weight bearing joints.

Irritable bowel syndrome   A common intestinal condition characterized by abdominal pain and cramps; changes in bowel movements (diarrhea, constipation, or both); gassiness; bloating; nausea; and other symptoms.

Knee flexion   Bending the knee joint.

Knee extension   Straightening the knee joint.

Lumbar extension   The spine bends backward.

Lumbar flexion   The spine bends forward.

Lumbar lateral flexion   The spine bending to the side, left or right.

Lumbar rotation   The spine twisting to the side, left or right.

Midfoot   The area in the middle of the foot, including the cuboid, navicular medial cuneiform, intermediate cuneiform, and lateral cuneiform bones and surrounding soft tissues.

Midsole   The shoe sole between the outer sole (which contacts the ground) and the shoe upper.

Mineral A substance that does not contain carbon and is widely distributed in nature. Minerals play an important role in human metabolism.

Motor Carrying motor impulses away from a central organ or part, as a nerve that conducts impulses from the central nervous system to the periphery of the body.

Negative adaptation To get weaker with or without stress.

Neurology The medical science that deals with the nervous system and the disorders affecting it.

Nutrition The science of food. The process of ingesting, digesting, transporting, absorbing, utilizing, and excreting nutrients.

Obesity An abnormal accumulation of body fat, usually 20 percent or more over an individual's ideal body weight.

Orthotic An orthopedic appliance designed to support, straighten or change, and control the position and/or function of the foot.

Outsole The shoe sole where the foot meets the ground.

Overpronation An excessive inward rolling motion of the foot outside the safe range while standing, walking, or running.

Oversupination An excessive outward rolling motion of the foot outside the safe range during standing, walking, or running.

Oxygen A nonmetallic element that exists in its free form as a colorless, odorless gas and makes up about 21 percent of the Earth's atmosphere.

Pain An unpleasant sensation occurring in varying degrees of severity as a consequence of injury, disease, or emotional disorder.

Painful inflammation Inflammation that is above normal. Stimulates the sensation of pain in the brain.

Pancreas   A gland that lies behind the stomach and next to the duodenum. The pancreas releases glucagon, insulin, and some of the enzymes that aid digestion.

Parkinson's disease   A progressive nervous disease occurring most often after the age of fifty, associated with the destruction of brain cells that produce dopamine, and characterized by muscular tremors, slowing of movement, partial facial paralysis, peculiarity of gait and posture, and weakness.

Plantar flexion   Toe-down motion of the foot at the ankle.

Plastic deformity   When the spring deforms, stores energy, then fails to return to its original shape, and in doing so only releases part of the stored energy.

Plyometrics   A type of exercise designed to produce fast, powerful movements and improve the functioning of the nervous system, generally for the purpose of improving performance in sports.

Positive adaptation   To get stronger under stress.

Pronation   A normal, slight inward rolling motion the foot makes during a walking or running stride.

Proteins   Any of a large number of substances present in milk, eggs, meat, etc., which are necessary as part of the food of human beings and animals.

Reproductive system   The complex of male or female gonads, associated ducts, and external genitalia concerned with sexual reproduction.

Resistance exercise   Any training that uses a resistance to the force of muscular contraction.

Respiration   The exchange of oxygen and carbon dioxide between the atmosphere and the body cells, including ventilation, diffusion of oxygen and carbon dioxide, and transport of oxygen to and carbon dioxide from body cells.

Respiratory system   The integrated system of organs involved in the intake and exchange of oxygen and carbon dioxide between the body and the environment and including the nasal passages, larynx, trachea, bronchial tubes, and lungs.

Restless leg syndrome   A condition that is characterized by an irresistible urge to move one's body to stop uncomfortable or odd sensations.

Safe range   The range of foot rolling from supination to pronation without abnormal stress and strain on the body.

Sensory nerve   A nerve that passes impulses from receptors toward or to the central nervous system.

Shank   The bridge between the heel and the ball area of a shoe. The higher the heel, the higher, narrower, and more curved the shank.

Silent inflammation   Inflammation that is above normal but not acute enough to stimulate the sensation of pain in the brain.

Spark   A flash of light, especially a flash produced by an electrical discharge.

Spring   An elastic object used to store mechanical energy.

Spring loading   When the body impacts the ground, compressing the human spring.

Spring suspension system   The muscles that suspend the arch of the foot, peroneus longus, peroneus brevis, tibialis posterior, and tibialis anterior.

Spring training   Exercise that engages the loading and unloading of the human spring.

Spring unloading   When the body lifts from the ground, decompressing the human spring.

Supination   A normal, slight outward rolling motion of the foot and ankle during a walking or running stride.

Supplements   Usually, dietary substances used to augment, enhance, or enrich the nutritional status of a patient.

Toe box   The *roof* of the toe end of the shoe. Its shape and height are determined by the shoe's design, and is important to comfort and fit.

Ultimate or failure strength   The maximum stress maintained in a body prior to its rupture.

Unsafe range   The range of foot rolling that results in either overrolling in pronation or supination outside the safe range. Rolling of the foot in this range results in negative stress and strain on the body.

Vertebra   Any of the bones or cartilaginous segments forming the spinal column.

Vitamin   Any of a group of unrelated organic substances occurring in many foods in small amounts and necessary in trace amounts for the normal metabolic functioning of the body.

Yield   The maximum force allowed before plastic deformity.

Index